Personal Finance

FOR BUSY PEOPLE

D0731330

Other Busy People Books

Taxes for Busy People
Robert Cooke

Time Management for Busy People
Roberta Roesch

Stress Management for Busy People
Carol Turkington

Word 97 for Busy People
Christian Crumlish

Windows 95 for Busy People
Ron Mansfield

Office 97 for Busy People
Steve Nelson

Quicken 98 for Busy People
Peter Weverka

Personal Finance

FOR BUSY PEOPLE

The Book to Use When There's No Time to Lose!

Robert A. Cooke

McGraw-Hill

New York   San Francisco   Washington, D.C.   Auckland   Bogotá
Caracas   Lisbon   London   Madrid   Mexico City   Milan
Montreal   New Delhi   San Juan   Singapore
Sydney   Tokyo   Toronto

Library of Congress Catalog Card Number: 98-065407

McGraw-Hill

A Division of The **McGraw·Hill** Companies

Copyright © 1998 by Robert Cooke. All rights reserved. Printed in the United States of America. Except as permitted under the United States Copyright Act of 1976, no part of this publication may be reproduced or distributed in any form or by any means, or stored in a database or retrieval system, without the prior written permission of the publisher.

1 2 3 4 5 6 7 8 9 0 DOC/DOC 9 0 3 2 1 0 9 8

ISBN 0-07-012556-2

The sponsoring editor for this book was Susan Barry,
the editor was Shirley Covington,
the assistant editor was Griffin Hansbury,
the editing supervisor was Rick Soldin,
the designer was Ted Mader Associates,
and the production supervisor was Clare Stanley.
It was set in Adobe Garamond by Electronic Publishing Services, Inc.

Printed and bound by R. R. Donnelley & Sons Company.

McGraw-Hill books are available at special quantity discounts to use as premiums and sales promotions, or for use in corporate training programs. For more information, please write to the Director of Special Sales, McGraw-Hill, 11 West 19th Street, New York, NY 10011. Or contact your local bookstore.

This publication is designed to provide accurate and authoritative information in regard to the subject matter covered. It is sold with the understanding that the publisher is not engaged in rendering legal, accounting, or other professional service. If legal advice or other expert assistance is required, the services of a competent professional person should be sought.

—from a declaration of principles jointly adopted by a committee
of the American Bar Association and a committee of publishers

Contents at a glance

1 How to Squeeze More Out of Present Income 1

2 More Places Where You Can Find Money 25

3 Protect Your Earning Power from Calamities 43

4 Protect Your Health—Keep Your Access to Medical Care 63

5 Emergency Money and Savings for Short-term Needs 75

6 Real Estate—Where You Can Stash Your
Long-term Money 89

7 Make Your Money Grow: Relatively Safe Investments 105

8 Common Stocks—Can You Make Money in
the Stock Market? 121

9 Mutual Funds (A Better Idea) and Other Investments 143

10 The Future—College, Retirement, and More Help 161

Appendix 183

Index 187

About the Author 197

Contents

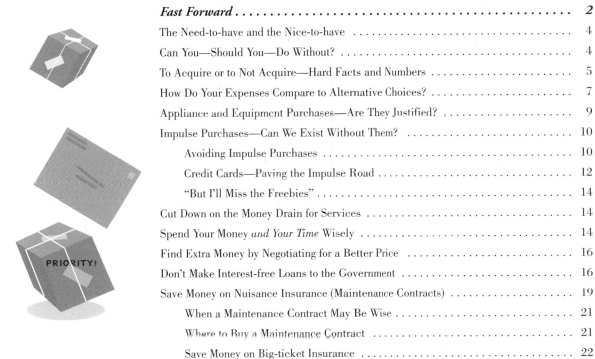

Introduction xvii

1   How to Squeeze More Out of Present Income   1

Fast Forward **2**

The Need-to-have and the Nice-to-have   4

Can You—Should You—Do Without?   4

To Acquire or to Not Acquire—Hard Facts and Numbers   5

How Do Your Expenses Compare to Alternative Choices?   7

Appliance and Equipment Purchases—Are They Justified?   9

Impulse Purchases—Can We Exist Without Them?   10

　　Avoiding Impulse Purchases   10

　　Credit Cards—Paving the Impulse Road   12

　　"But I'll Miss the Freebies"   14

Cut Down on the Money Drain for Services   14

Spend Your Money *and Your Time* Wisely   14

Find Extra Money by Negotiating for a Better Price   16

Don't Make Interest-free Loans to the Government   16

Save Money on Nuisance Insurance (Maintenance Contracts)   19

　　When a Maintenance Contract May Be Wise   21

　　Where to Buy a Maintenance Contract   21

　　Save Money on Big-ticket Insurance   22

More Ways to Save Dollars   23

2   More Places Where You Can Find Money   25

Fast Forward **26**

Spend Less to Finance Your Purchases   27

　　Credit Cards   27

　　Easy Terms from Your Friendly Retail Store   28

　　Consumer Loans from Banks and Finance Companies   29

　　Home Equity Financing   29

Buy or Lease? The Right Answer Can Save Significantly 32

    Example: Leasing an Automobile 32

    Lease and Rental of Other Equipment 37

How to Motivate Yourself to Control Your Money 38

    Keep Some Fun in Your Life (Reward Yourself) 38

    Include Your 401(k) Plan in Your Planning 41

3   **Protect Your Earning Power from Calamities** **43**

    Fast Forward **44**

Who Pays the Bills If You Are Injured or Sick and Can't Work? 45

    Depend on the Government? Ha! 45

    Disability Insurance from Commercial Insurance Companies 46

Who Pays the Bills If You Are Dead? 51

    Here Is Basic, Unembellished Life Insurance 51

    Embellished Life Insurance 52

    More Confusion: The Varieties of Cash-value Life Insurance 56

    How Much Life Insurance Do You Need? 57

    The Bottom Line—What Should You Do About Life Insurance? 59

    Where to Find Advice 59

In a Few Words: Life Insurance and Disability Insurance 61

4   **Protect Your Health—Keep Your Access to Medical Care** **63**

    Fast Forward **64**

What Is the Best Kind of Medical Insurance? 65

    What Kind of Insurance Can I Get? 65

    Your Doctor and Hospital Bill the Insurance Company 66

Coverage from Your Employer 68

Health Maintenance Organizations (HMOs)—Probably Here to Stay 68

    How an HMO Operates 69

    The Upside of HMOs 69

    The Downside of HMOs 69

    Which Should You Buy—HMO or Conventional Health Insurance? 70

    What to Do If You Cannot Find Insurance or HMO Coverage Because

        You Have a Medical Problem 70

How to Handle Health Insurance When You Change Employers 71

How to Handle Health Insurance If You Quit Your Job 71

Medicare (for Those 65 and Over) 72

How Do You Sign Up? 72

Do You Need Supplemental Insurance? 72

What About Medicare HMOs? 73

Long-term Care Insurance 73

Rely on the Government? 73

Are You Eligible for Medicaid? 74

5   Emergency Money and Savings for Short-term Needs 75

Fast Forward *76*

Emergencies? We Have Insurance 77

How Much Should You Keep in Your Emergency Fund? 77

Possible Emergencies for Which You Should Be Financially Prepared. 77

Upcoming Expenses You Know About and Anticipate 78

Where to Keep Your Emergency Funds 80

What Type of Bank Account(s) Should You Keep Your Money In? 81

Money Market Funds 84

Earn 18 Percent on Your Money with No Risk 85

Emergency Funds versus Short-term Investments 87

Investment Comes in Two Distinct Flavors 87

6   Real Estate—Where You Can Stash Your Long-term Money 89

Fast Forward *90*

How Long Is It to Harvest Time? What Is Long Term? 91

What Is Your Risk Tolerance? 92

Real Estate: A Good Place to Build Your Nest Egg 93

The Best Real Estate Investment—Your Residence (Usually) 94

The Benefits of Owning Your House 94

The Advantages of Renting Your House (The Disadvantages of Owning It) 95

The Costs of Buying and Selling Your House 95

Using a Real Estate Broker or Agent 96

Where and How to Borrow the Money You Need to Buy a House 97

Should You Take on a Mortgage Even If You Don't Have to? 97

Variable-Rate or Fixed-Rate Mortgage? 98

Should You Sign a Balloon Mortgage? 98

Investing In and Owning Rental Property 100

Make Money from Rental Property and Cut Your Taxes 100

Some Other Considerations About Rental Property Ownership 102

Real Estate Investment Trusts (REITs) 103

7   Make Your Money Grow: Relatively Safe Investments 105

Fast Forward *106*

Money Your Money Earns 107

How Much Risk Should You Take? 108

Safe Investments: Government Bonds and Similar Places to Put Your Money 108

Savings Bonds Today (Series EE) 109

Series HH Savings Bonds 110

Other Ways You Can Loan Money to the U.S. Government 111

What Is Yield and How Is It Calculated? 114

IOU Prices, IOU Yields: Which Is Which? 115

Where and How to Buy U.S. Treasury Securities 116

Bonds Issued by State and Local Governments 116

Should You Buy Tax-exempt Bonds? 116

Are Municipal Bonds Safe? 118

Notes and Bonds Issued by Corporations (Not Quite the U.S. Treasury) 119

Why Buy Bonds Issued by Corporations? 119

Will the Corporate Bonds Be Good When They Mature? 119

Can I Get My Money Out Before Maturity? 119

What Are Convertible Bonds? 119

Are "Junk" Bonds a Good Deal? 120

8   Common Stocks—Can You Make Money in the Stock Market? 121

Fast Forward *122*

The Corporation—It Makes Sharing Ownership Easy 123

Who Gets Paid First (Priorities)? 125

Money Invested in Stocks Should Earn Money (Dividends) 126

Net Income and Dividends 126

More Money for the Stockholders (Capital Gains) 127

Watch the Dividend Dates 128

Initial Public Offering (IPO) 129

What Is and Where Is the Stock Market? 129

Spread the Ownership Around (Stock Splits) 131

Preferred Stock 132

Convertibles 133

What Is the Right Price for a Stock? 133

Should You Invest in Stocks? 135

What Are the Risks and the Non-risks? History That Is Not

  Taught in the Tenth Grade 135

  Are We Protected Today from a Recurrence of 1929? 137

Where to Go for Help in Buying Stocks 138

Where Should You Buy Stocks? 138

  Full-service Brokers 138

  Commercial Banks 139

  Discount Brokers 139

  Deep Discount Brokers 139

  On-line Electronic Brokers 140

Stock Trading 140

Derivatives 141

What's Next? 142

9 **Mutual Funds (A Better Idea) and Other Investments** 143

 Fast Forward *144*

Mutual Funds: What They Are and How They Live 145

What Happens to the Earnings of the Mutual Fund? 148

Determining the Price of Mutual Fund Shares 148

Why Buy Shares of a Mutual Fund with Your Investment Money? 149

  You Avoid Having to Make Some Decisions 149

  Your Investments Will Be Spread Around 149

Why Many People Don't Invest in Mutual Funds 149

  Fees Involved When You Invest in Mutual Funds 150

  Large Mutual Funds Are Inflexible 151

Buy at the Wrong Time and Pay Income Tax on Your Own Money 152

Closed-end Funds 153

Other Varieties of Funds 153

  Real Estate Investment Trusts (REITs) 153

Real Estate Mutual Funds 154

Bond Funds 154

Index Mutual Funds 154

How to Buy Mutual Funds 155

Where to Go for More Help and Self-education on Mutual Funds 155

Annuities 158

Gold and Other Precious Metals 160

Coins, Collectibles, and Art 160

10   The Future—College, Retirement, and More Help **161**

Fast Forward *162*

Children, Smart or Not, Need Education 164

What Is Your Child's College Material Score? 164

How Much Time Do You Have? 164

How Bad Is the Situation? How Much Money Will You Need? 164

What Should You Do? 165

Apply for Scholarships, Grants, and Student Loans—Lots of Them 167

What Is Available in the Form of Grants and Scholarships? 169

Where to Invest Your Savings for Education 170

Some Help from the IRS (Really!) 172

What Your Offspring Can Contribute 174

Will You Ever Retire? How Will You Live? How Long Will You Live? 174

What Will Be the Source of Your Income? 175

How Much Do You Need to Put Away for Your Retirement? 177

The Future Is Here 179

Where to Go from Here? Do You Need Professional Help? 180

In Conclusion 181

Appendix. **183**

Tax Rate Table (For Determining Tax Bracket) 183

Computation of Interest Rate in Equipment Lease Contract 184

Instructions for Using Table in Figure A.2 for Estimating Interest Rates 184

Sources of More Information 185

Index 187

About the Author 197

Figures

1.1 Computation of Expense of Automobile Operation 6

1.2 Automobile versus Bus and Shoe Leather 8

1.3 Purchasing a Washer and Dryer versus Using the Laundromat 9

1.4 Effective (?) Use of Shopping Time by Archie 15

1.5 Avoid Loaning Free Money to Uncle Sam 18

1.6 Provide Your Own Maintenance Contracts 20

2.1 Computation of After-tax Interest Rate When Interest Is Deductible 30

2.2 Leasing versus Purchasing 36

2.3 Computation of Interest Charge in Rental/Purchase Arrangement 38

2.4 Calculation of Net Income and Essential Expenses for an Individual 39

2.5 Self-motivation and Saving Plan for an Individual 41

3.1 Comparison of Disability Income Insurance 49

3.2 Computation of Disability Insurance Needed 50

3.3 How Much Life Insurance Do You Need? 58

4.1 Health Insurance Pays and It Doesn't Pay 67

5.1 Form for Computing Emergency and Saving Funds Needed 80

5.2 Comparison of Bank Money Market Deposit Account to Money Market Fund 84

5.3 Winning Income from the Bank 86

6.1 Computation of After-tax Income from Rental Property Investment 102

7.1 Should an Individual Cash in Her EE Bonds or Exchange Them for HH Bonds? . . . 112

7.2 Computation of Taxable versus Tax-exempt Yield from Bonds 118

8.1 How Stock Splits Usually Behave 132

8.2 How to Compute the Price-earnings Ratio 134

9.1 Swimincash, Results of First Year 147

9.2 Effect of Dollar Cost Averaging 156

10.1 Savings Needed for College 166

10.2 Computation of Retirement Needs 178

A.1 Determination of Your Tax Bracket Percentage for Calculating
Federal Income Tax Effects 183

A.2 Table for Estimating Interest Charged in Lease/Purchase Agreement 185

INTRODUCTION

You're busy—probably busy making money. The dollars roll in, and they all roll out again. Despite raises and bonuses, there is always more month than there is paycheck. How do you reverse that, so there is some money left at the end of the month? Then, what do you do with that money so it grows into a respectable nest egg for retirement or the kids' educations? This book answers those questions, without wasting your time on extraneous discussions.

What This Book Will Do for You and How to Use It

You could find the answers to those questions in a college text on finance or a similar book, but where would you find the endless hours needed to wade through the doctrines and principles? In these pages, I've whittled away the needless recitations of theory and concentrated on the explanations of "how to . . ." How to squeeze extra money out of your present income; how to make sure emergencies don't obliterate your nest egg; and how to make your money grow safely. To help you learn the most in the shortest time, there are examples and calculations you can easily follow and adapt to your own situation. That is, there is much "how to" and little "why you should . . ."

I have also included a section of how to keep your college-bound kids from obliterating your retirement kitty. In more technical terms, there are rules to follow to make sure your family receives all the educational financial aid to which you are entitled.

If you are like most busy people, the nuts and bolts in this book are all you need to get started on a financial plan that will actually work. If you already have a nest egg (perhaps an inheritance), you may need the help of a professional financial planner. This book is also designed to help those in that situation. First, there are meaningful suggestions on how to choose that professional help. Second, the knowledge you gain from this book will give you a head start in understanding what your advisor is suggesting—and that will keep him or her alert—and honest.

In the years I practiced as a CPA, financial advisor, and confidant, I would sometimes try to help a client by straying into explanations of financial theory, but I was always brought up short by his or her request for "just the facts—please just tell me what to do." Those lessons from clients are what underlie this book.

With the great help from the editors and graphic designers at McGraw-Hill, this book does, I think, succeed in giving you just the facts and essentials.

Things You Might Want to Know About This Book

You can read this book in almost any order. If you already are astute or lucky enough to have more money than you spend, you can skip the first two chapters and zero in on how to invest that money—from government bonds (everyone should have some) to oil futures (only for your gambling money).

Confused by your insurance agent? There is specific help in understanding insurance in Chapters 3 and 4. Is owning rental real estate your cup of tea? That's covered in Chapter 6.

Besides a comprehensive table of contents and index, the book includes some special elements to help you spot the sections that can provide instant help.

Fast Forward

Every chapter begins with a section called *Fast Forward*. Each of these sections is, in effect, a book within a book—a built-in quick reference guide, summarizing the money-managing techniques explained and suggested in the chapter that follows. If you're already familiar with the techniques, the Fast Forward may be all you need to read of the particular chapter. (The Fast Forward acts as a check list of ideas you knew once, but have become buried in your brain's memory bank.)

Expert Advice

Timesaving tips, techniques, and worthwhile additions are all reported under the rubric of *Expert Advice*. (Look for the pensive scientist.) Force yourself to develop some good habits now, while it's still possible! These notes also give you the big picture and help you plan ahead.

Caution

Sometimes it's too easy to plunge ahead and fall down a manhole, resulting in lost hours and, worse, lost money. This icon will warn you about the care you should exercise when taking a course of action.

Definition

If you encounter words you don't recognize, look for this bodybuilder in the margin. *Definitions* point out important terms you might not reasonably know the meaning of. When necessary, definitions are strict and a little technical, but most of the time they're informal and conversational.

Margin Notes

Throughout the book, cross-references and other minor asides appear in margin notes like this one.

Let's Do It!

How to Squeeze More Out of Present Income

INCLUDES

- Setting priorities: the need-to-have and the nice-to-have
- Controlling impulse purchases
- Cut down on services
- Time is money, and vice versa
- Buying on the cheap: shopping and negotiating for cowards
- Don't make interest-free loans to the government

FAST FORWARD

- Set priorities. Distinguish between the need-to-have and the nice-to-have. *(pp. 3–9)*
  - What can you do without? Be honest with yourself, and make two lists of needs: (1) essentials and (2) nonessentials.
  - Are there less expensive alternatives?
  - Can you justify major expenditures? Put your reasons (including hard numbers) on paper.
- Avoid impulse purchases. *(pp. 10–14)*
  - Impose a cooling-off period of at least overnight.
  - Use a credit card only when necessary (for example, for travel reservations and rental cars).
  - Set up credit card rules for yourself. Examples: No more than three cards, pay balance within grace period, use only for specific purposes.
- Reduce services. (That does not mean doing without.) Example: Reduce the frequency of lawn maintenance, house cleaning, and similar assistance. *(p. 14)*
- Determine the value of your time. Then you can tell if the purchase of a labor-saving device or service is cost-effective. (Much depends on how you can use the time you can free up.) *(p. 14)*
- Be a better shopper. Take the time to comparison shop only when the possible savings are significant. Hate to negotiate? Try just leaving the sales room without buying—it often works. *(p. 16)*
- Don't make interest-free loans to the government. Keep *your* money working for *you*. Learn the IRS rules that can put extra money in your pocket. *(pp. 16–19)*

For most of us, financial planning is required when someone has surplus cash and needs to determine the best place to keep it or the best financial products to buy with it. But that someone does not include us. We picture ourselves as among the great unwashed who watch our money come in and quickly leave again, and often it leaves before it arrives (as in *credit cards*). That mental picture of an individual with surplus cash is valid occasionally, but there is only a handful of people for whom money floats down out of the sky and piles up around them. The rest of us have to work at making the green stuff accumulate.

Some individuals live in the false bliss of believing that once they receive that promotion and increase in income the accumulation will be automatic. It isn't so. Without some financial planning, the individual with a $2,000,000 salary will spend $2,200,000 just as surely as the person who earns $10,000 will spend $11,000.

Regardless of your income, then, you need to find extra cash from within it. In simple words, you need to save some of what you earn. The financial world abounds in such aphorisms as, "pay yourself first," or "put money aside for . . . (the rainy day, retirement, etc.)." Sure, these generalities are good advice, but they don't get the job done.

This chapter and the next one do tell you how to get the job done, how to squeeze real cash out of your income. We start by looking at some choices about your cash outflow that you should make, and then we cover the ways you can make these choices in an unemotional manner. The productive use you should make of this squeezed-out cash comes in later chapters.

The Need-to-have and the Nice-to-have

People survived 150 years ago without automobiles, modern plumbing, telephones, television, stereos, microwaves, food processors, and $150 athletic shoes. Could anyone survive without these "necessities" of today? You could. Some people do, either by choice or because of where they were born. Should *you* live without these components of modern life?

Can You—Should You—Do Without?

Obviously, a modern invention such as a telephone has become a real necessity. Indeed, there are some jobs that require an employee to have a telephone. But do you need the pager and the cellular phone? Do you really need a video telephone? (Yes, a *few* people really do need those technical marvels for their work.)

Not many houses had any plumbing 150 years ago. That is still true in remote regions, but in metropolitan areas, zoning laws and health departments have changed plumbing from a convenience to not only a necessity but a legal requirement. Yet there are still choices. Before World War II, most houses had one bathroom. Now we think in terms of multiple bathrooms. If you have four teenagers in your household, viewing multiple bathrooms as a necessity is obviously justified. However, does a couple with one eight-year-old child really need four and a half bathrooms?

We could discuss many accouterments of modern life in generalities such as this, but how can we sort out the need-to-haves from the nice-to-haves in an objective manner? How can we reduce buying and spending decisions to facts that will help us make money-conserving choices?

To answer those questions, let's consider an item that almost all of us—with the exception of residents of cities with good public transport systems— have or have had at some time.

To Acquire or to Not Acquire—Hard Facts and Numbers

Probably no item is considered more essential in modern America than the automobile, even though some people get along without one. What follows is an analysis of the justification for owning a passenger vehicle. This may sound like a waste of time, given that most of us consider a car, van, pickup truck, or utility vehicle to be a necessity in our world. However, you can use parts of this analysis to justify or fail to justify the ownership of many conveniences, gadgets, and toys.

In Figure 1.1, we generate some facts to use in deciding if you should continue to own an automobile or sell it to generate more cash. The major fact that you need to know is how much it costs to operate the vehicle. Although the computation shown in Figure 1.1 works out to 40 cents per mile, you may have different numbers to plug into these calculations, which will, of course, result in a different cost per mile.

These calculations are self-explanatory and need little other comment, except for the last item: interest on the cost. That number of $6,000 assumes you borrowed the $20,000 with which you bought the vehicle at approximately 11 percent interest and repaid it in 60 monthly installments. What if, instead, you paid cash for the vehicle by cashing in $20,000 of corporate bonds you owned and on which you received 11 percent interest. Now you no longer have that interest income flowing into your hands. That lost interest income is just as much a cost of owning the vehicle as is paying interest to the finance company. Financial experts call this an *opportunity cost*—you have lost the opportunity to earn interest (or dividends or capital gains) if you use your cash to buy an automobile.

Cost of automobile when purchased	$20,000	
Subtract value after five years of use	3,000	
Net cost of auto	$17,000	
Number of miles you expect to drive vehicle	100,000	
Cost per mile (cost ÷ miles)		$0.17
Cost of oil change	$ 30	
Divide by miles between oil changes	3,000	
Cost per mile (cost ÷ miles)		0.01
Cost of repairs, tires, etc. over the five years you own vechicle	$ 5,000	
Number of miles you expect to drive vehicle	100,000	
Cost per mile (cost ÷ miles)		0.05
Cost of gas, per gallon	$1.50	
Average miles per gallon	20	
Cost per mile (cost ÷ miles)		0.08
Cost of insurance over five years	$ 2,500	
Number of miles you expect to drive vehicle	100,000	
Cost per mile (cost ÷ miles)		0.03
Cost of interest on $20,000 five-year loan	$ 6,000	
Number of miles you expect to drive vehicle	100,000	
Cost per mile (cost ÷ miles)		0.06
Total cost per mile		$0.40

Figure 1.1 Computation of Expense of Automobile Operation

EXPERT ADVICE

For this to be a valid comparison of buying versus renting, you should pay yourself payments of principal and interest—just as you would pay the finance company. Then, buy back the corporate bonds (or other investment) with the money you pay yourself. If you don't follow this procedure, 60 months down the road, you will find yourself with a well-worn car and $20,000 less in your investment account. (Actually, you will be out far more than $20,000, because you also will not have the interest you should have paid yourself.)

How Do Your Expenses Compare to Alternative Choices?

The use of money costs money, regardless of whether it is your money or the bank's money.

The obvious alternative would be to buy a different vehicle. What if you purchased a less expensive vehicle? If you did this same computation using a vehicle costing $10,000, your cost per mile would be only 27 cents. However, your repair costs may be higher, and there is the intangible cost of riding in a vehicle that may not be as safe as a more expensive one.

Another alternative is to use the figure of 40 cents per mile to compare other means of transportation. Obviously, you cannot ride in a taxicab or limousine for 40 cents a mile, but how about the bus, trolley, or subway? On the surface, these might look like money-saving alternatives, but are they?

Figure 1.2 considers alternatives and develops a savings of $10 per day if you own and use your own vehicle. This calculation does assume that your time is valuable and can be converted into additional cash income, as is certainly true for professionals in a practice such as law, accounting, engineering, and so on. For these folk, additional time spent at the job can equal more billable hours. And for most self-employed people, time at work does bring in more cash (eventually), so there definitely is a relationship between time and money.

Of course, if your extra time doesn't have value, then there is a saving in using the bus, trolley, or subway for commuting.

> Assume your commute to work is 40 miles each way. The out-of-pocket expenses of the bus or trolley are less, but there are other factors:
>
> Costs of bus commuting:
>
> | | | |
> |---|---|---|
> | Bus fare | | $ 5.00 |
> | Time waiting for bus | 0.50 hours | |
> | Extra travel time (bus is slow due to stops) | 1.00 hour | |
> | Total time | 1.50 hours | |
> | Value of your time, per hour | $30.00 | |
> | Cost of time (1.5 hours × $30) | | 45.00 |
> | Total cost of bus transportation | | 50.00 |
>
> Subtract cost of automobile commute:
>
> | | | |
> |---|---|---|
> | 80 miles @ 40 cents per mile | 32.00 | |
> | Parking | 8.00 | |
> | Total cost of automobile transportation | | 40.00 |
> | Daily saving from commuting by own automobile | | $10.00 |

Figure 1.2 Automobile versus Bus and Shoe Leather

What if you are an employee who is paid a fixed salary for a 40- (or 50- or 60-) hour week? The relationship between time and money isn't so obvious, but try to determine some number of dollars per hour based on the following thoughts and considerations:

- Can you perform better on your job if you arrive early and are ready to start when the bell rings? Does your employer reward performance?
- Does arriving early and leaving later give you time for informal chitchat with those higher on the corporate ladder? Will that visibility help you climb the ladder?
- Can you use the time saved for education, either at night school or by listening to training audio tapes in your car?

Time saved equals money provided you put the time to productive use.

You probably can think of other considerations that apply to your job situation. For all, though, the key is what you do with the time saved.

Appliance and Equipment Purchases—Are They Justified?

Here's an application of this procedure to a household decision: Should you purchase a washer and dryer or continue to lug the dirty clothes to the Laundromat? Figure 1.3 follows the format of the automobile analysis and results in only five cents difference between the weekly cost of buying the machines and putting up with the hassle of a Laundromat. Your own figures, particularly for the cost of electricity and water, may be quite different from those in Figure 1.3.

Purchase, computation of weekly cost:		
Cost of washer and dryer	$700.00	
Life in weeks	150.00	
Cost per week ($700 ÷ 150)		$ 4.67
Interest		2.22
Repairs ($100 over 3 years)		1.35
Electricity per week		3.00
Water per week		1.00
Total cost per week		12.24
Laundromat, weekly cost:		
Washer, 4 loads @ $1	4.00	
Dryer, 4 loads @ $2	8.00	
Total cost per week		12.00
Weekly saving by purchasing washer and dryer		$ 0.24

Figure 1.3 Purchasing a Washer and Dryer versus Using the Laundromat

Don't assume that if you continue with the Laundromat you can put the $700 to work in an investment. Initially you can, but the theory goes that you would have to liquidate the investment to have the quarters to feed the Laundromat machines.

Theory aside, however, putting the $700 into an investment might be a self-discipline procedure. (Use your pocket change for the Laundromat and keep the $700 invested.)

Impulse Purchases—Can We Exist Without Them?

Our society flourishes because of strong economic activity. What is economic activity? It's people and companies buying and selling various materials, products, and services. Do you contribute to this economic activity? If you need food and shelter, you do. Are you obligated to contribute as much as possible by buying everything you can possibly afford? Of course not. But you and I are constantly bombarded with enticements from those who would have us spend all we earn—and more—by buying their wares or services. How do you thwart these enticements, so that you have something left for yourself and for your investment?

Avoiding Impulse Purchases

Never buy anything you did not intend to buy when you entered the store, opened the catalog, or logged on to your Internet service.

I used to preach that principle daily to my friend Mary, but she continued to spend her paycheck within a day after payday on sale items, new products, and things that just looked attractive. Her answer to my objections were that she saved money by buying the goods on sale, she had to try the new items, and the attractive items did not cost much, anyway. So she was always broke.

Now, however, she has changed. She no longer shops that way, and she has a tidy sum put away for emergencies and retirement. What changed her?

I'm not sure, but one evening, when she was penniless just before payday, she asked me to help her make her paycheck stretch. Although I was afraid it might be futile, we sat at her kitchen table and made up two shopping lists. The first was of essentials: milk, bread, cereal, soup, and other basic food. It also included some have-to-have items: a snow shovel and a pair of gloves. (The snow was falling, it was 15 degrees, and she had neither of those basic needs for Boston weather.) These were the items she would purchase the next evening.

The second list we made up was titled "deferred needs." It included a new clock radio, a coat, and a nonstick electric frying pan. These could be deferred because the alarm on her old clock radio worked, but the radio part didn't. She had a coat, but it was becoming somewhat worn, so she needed a new one to keep up appearances at her office. Her old nonstick frying pan was no longer nonstick. It could be cleaned up with a lot of elbow grease, but the next overcooked (burned) dinner would probably end its life. Did Mary run right out and fill these needs at the mall? No. We agreed that she would price the replacement items in at least two stores, and then watch for sales. If she found no sales in the next two months, she would buy them at the store or mail-order house that had the best regular price.

She carried this deferred needs list with her at all times, adding to it when she realized she had an essential need and deleting items for which she had found a good deal. She eventually enhanced the procedure by anticipating needs six to twelve months in advance. That put her in a position to take advantage of end-of-season sales.

Mary found that the hardest part of the procedure was the absolute requirement to follow this rule: Unless the item was on a "needs" or "deferred needs" list, she did not buy it, no matter how good a deal was being offered or how enticing a promotional display was. In other words: *no* impulse purchases. She purchased only those items she had determined she needed when she was away from any stimulation that said "buy me."

Later, Mary kept a third list, consisting of nonessential-but-would-enjoy items. You see, she didn't live in a suspended state of denial of all pleasure. She actually did acquire some of these luxuries—gadgets, shows, travel, and so on. But they were acquired in a controlled manner. Specifically, she set goals. If she wanted a $100 luxury, she made herself wait until she had stashed five times that amount into her savings plan. When she decided on a $1,000 cruise, she made herself wait until she had put another $5,000 into her investment plan.

Keeping a list of nonnecessities also accomplished what this story illustrates: In the spring rains, she decided she would like to have an electric umbrella. (It compacted into a six-inch tube and it unfurled at a push of a button, aided by a battery-powered electric motor; it sold for $79.95.) However, when she reached the savings goal that permitted her to buy it, she had cooled to the idea. Instead, she bought a basic $8.95 umbrella that did just as good a job in keeping her dry. She spent the $71 difference on theater tickets. (Remember, she had already reached a savings goal.)

EXPERT ADVICE

- *Keep three lists of what you need:*

  1. *Essentials you must have right away, such as food, cleaning supplies, mechanical repairs and maintenance on your vehicle and appliances, and similar basic requirements of modern life.*

  2. *Those items you need soon but have some time in which to shop and compare.*

  3. *Luxuries you think you would like, along with a goal of how much you must have saved before you can purchase the luxury item.*

Credit Cards—Paving the Impulse Road

After reading this far, you're probably expecting the advice to cut up all your credit cards. But cut them all up? If your job requires travel, you will feel pretty awkward hitchhiking to a business conference in Chicago because you can't buy an airplane ticket, rent a car, or reserve a hotel room. If you have 20 of the things, by all means, cut up 17 of them. Keep only three at the most, and be sure to keep those with no annual charge and with a grace period during which you can pay for purchases without incurring a finance charge. Not only should you cut up the other credit cards, but you should notify the issuers that you are canceling the account. (Do not just telephone; send a written notification by certified mail.)

Even if you don't need a plastic card for business, not having even one of them can cost you. If you travel for pleasure, the credit card may be essential. It's also appropriate to use it when an opportunity presents itself, but you have only $13 in your pocket and no checkbook.

To continue the Mary example, this happened to her. When she found an electric skillet on sale for half price, she had only $1.56 in her pocket and, as usual, did not carry her checkbook with her. So her credit card allowed her to take advantage of the sale on an item that was *already* on her "needs" list.

EXPERT ADVICE

Keep a list of every item you charge to a credit card, with a running total for the card's billing period. Every time you charge an item on your credit card, record it on the list and update the total. Keep the list with your file of monthly bills and treat that total just as you do your mortgage payment or condo rent—as a "must pay" on a certain date.

Do not be enticed into running up a balance at a very low interest rate. If you receive an offer for a card that charges only 5 or 6 percent, read the fine print. It is probably a six-month introductory rate, after which you will be hit with the usual 14 to 20 percent interest rate. What the issuer hopes is that you won't read the fine print, so you will charge, and charge more, to your card, thinking that you can easily pay it off later. Then when it's later and the interest rate has tripled, you will have enough trouble paying the interest charges, let alone the cost of your purchases.

Avoid late charges. If your due date for payment is the fifth of the month, you are paid on the first, and you wait to pay the bill until your paycheck is deposited, you may quite frequently be hit with a late charge *and* interest charges. Solution: Send in the minimum payment on the day you receive the statement, which will ensure you escape any late fees. Then send the balance as soon as you can cover the check, preferably within the grace period.

Summary of Credit Card Rules

- *Use no more than three credit cards.*
- *If possible, use only credit cards that charge no annual fee and provide a grace period for payment without incurring finance charges.*
- *Do not charge anything to the credit card unless you have the cash with which to pay for it (or for which you know your employer will reimburse you).*
- *Pay the balance in full before the end of the grace period.*

"But I'll Miss the Freebies"

Do you have one or more of the credit cards that generate points or miles or some other type of premium and that charge no annual fee? Go ahead and use it for all your expenditures *IF* you have the discipline to use the credit only if the expenditure is on your first or second list (i.e., you have the cash to cover the charges). Also, be forewarned that credit card issuers are not happy with those who earn premiums but pay no interest or other charges. Don't be surprised if your card is suddenly canceled one day.

Cut Down on the Money Drain for Services

If you're busy earning money, then some services are essential. If you don't have time to take care of your lawn and gardens, a lawn-care service is a must if you are to avoid a citation from the city for a lawn that looks like a rain forest. But do you have to have service every week? If you reduce the service to every two weeks, you won't win an award for the best lawn in the neighborhood, but you will have more cash left in your bank account. And that cash will help finance your retirement (or your kid's college). The best-lawn award will provide nothing for you in your old age.

Spend Your Money *and Your Time* Wisely

Example: Archie was a real estate agent, and his success was due mainly to the inordinate amount of time he devoted to his profession. To better manage his time and impress his clients, he decided he needed a cellular telephone. About the same time, his briefcase disintegrated, so replacing it was in order.

He called the phone company and ordered the cellular telephone and service. Then he spent three hours checking out the price of briefcases in four retail stores. Was that a wise use of his time? Figure 1.4 tells the story.

Purchase of briefcase:		
List price of briefcase in luggage store		$ 150.00
Subtract, discounted price, in fourth store visited		125.00
Savings from "shopping"		25.00
Divide by 3 hours used shopping to compute savings per hour		$ 8.33
Acquisition of cellular telephone service:		
From local telephone company		
Price of cellular telephone, as purchased		$ 50.00
Service, per month	$75.00	
Multiply by expected life, in months, before something better comes along	36.00	
Cost of 36 months of service		2,700.00
Total cost, phone and service, for 36 months		$2,750.00
Available from competing cellular company (but Archie did not check its pricing):		
Price of cellular telephone, as purchased		$ 150.00
Service (identical to above), per month	$50.00	
Multiply by expected life before something better comes along, in months	36.00	
Cost of 36 months of service		1,800.00
Total cost, phone and service, for 36 months		$1,950.00
Summary:		
Cost of cellular service as purchased from local telephone company		$2,750.00
Subtract cost of similar service from competitor		1,950.00
Saving if Archie had shopped cellular service		800.00
Savings yield per hour if Archie had used the same 3 hours to call several cellular providers instead of briefcase merchants		$ 266.67
Did Archie spend his time wisely, saving $8.33 per hour instead of $266.67 per hour?		

Figure 1.4 Effective (?) Use of Shopping Time by Archie

Find Extra Money by Negotiating for a Better Price

You may be one of the many people who are uncomfortable negotiating for a lower price, and that discomfort is quite understandable. However, some merchants expect and live by negotiation. Examples are automobile dealers who do not subscribe to the one-price system, used-merchandise stores, surplus stores, and flea markets.

EXPERT ADVICE

If you're reluctant to offer a lower price than what is marked, try this: Show a great deal of interest in the item, making sure a salesperson is aware of your interest. Then reluctantly start to leave. Often, this action will bring forth an offer of a lower price from the merchant without your having to say anything.

Although negotiation usually will not work in a Wal-Mart or similar store, it may if you find damaged merchandise in the stock. Offer a lower price that is consistent with the damage. The manager may find that accepting the price is more expedient and profitable than filing freight damage claims, returning the merchandise to the manufacturer or to a "scratch-and-dent" outlet, or going through other hassles. The downside is that you will have to wait while the salesperson finds the manager who has the decision authority.

Don't Make Interest-free Loans to the Government

Many people are guilty of this—sending money off to Uncle Sam when they could hold onto it and earn interest on it. If you consistently receive a large refund of your federal income tax after you file your return, you are *giving* interest money to the government, and neither the president nor the IRS will send you a thank-you note.

Example: In 1996, the total tax on Sharon's tax return (before subtracting her withheld tax) was $6,000. Although her salary and deductions in 1997 looked to be the same as in 1996, she had sold some investments in January 1997 that resulted in $15,000 of capital gains tax, so she estimated that her 1997 tax would be about $21,000. To be certain that she would not owe any tax on April 15, she had asked her employer to withhold $2,000 out of each monthly paycheck, beginning in January 1997.

However, all she needed to pay by withholding (or by estimated tax) and still be within the requirements of the law was $6,000—the amount of her prior year's tax. She could have put the amount that her employer withheld into a money market fund and paid the extra $15,000 on April 15, 1998. Figure 1.5 computes what she lost by not following this alternative.

Although this situation, in which Sharon had about $15,000 in capital gains, is extreme, the same holds true if you routinely receive a tax refund of hundreds of dollars. Over time, if you continue with overwithholding, the interest you give to Uncle Sam can be significant. For instance, if you overpay your tax during the year by overwithholding or by paying too much in estimated payments by $5,000 per year, the lost interest to you over 10 years at 5 percent is $2,534. The solution: Claim enough additional deductions on a Form W-4 to eliminate or substantially reduce your refunds. To compute the additional exemptions, divide your expected overpayment of tax by $2,500.

CAUTION

Be aware that if you claim more than 10 exemptions, your employer must report that to the IRS. However, that does not mean that the IRS will automatically come knocking on your door. If you have paid your taxes as due in the past few years, you probably will not hear from anyone at the IRS.

How is this possible? There are two reasons: First, the IRS says you should have enough withheld (or pay enough estimated tax) so that you owe no more than $500 when you file your tax return on April 15. However, the tax law also says that there is no penalty for not having enough withheld or paid by estimated taxes *if* you pay at least the amount of your total tax for the previous year.

Date	Amount Sharon sent to the IRS	Amount she should have sent to the IRS	Amount she could have put into money market fund	Interest on funds in money market account
January 97	$1,750	$500	$ 1,250	
February 97	1,750	500	1,250	$ 5.21
March 97	1,750	500	1,250	10.44
April 97	1,750	500	1,250	15.69
May 97	1,750	500	1,250	20.96
June 97	1,750	500	1,250	26.26
July 97	1,750	500	1,250	31.58
August 97	1,750	500	1,250	36.92
September 97	1,750	500	1,250	42.28
October 97	1,750	500	1,250	47.66
November 97	1,750	500	1,250	53.07
December 97	1,750	500	1,250	58.50
January 98				63.95
February 98				64.22
March 98				64.49
April 98				32.38
Totals			$15,000	$573.60

Sharon legally kept $574 of interest that the IRS would rather have had. Actually, she earned a few more dollars of interest, as she wrote the check to the IRS (on April 15, 1998) on her money market account, so she earned interest until the IRS processed and deposited her check.

Figure 1.5 Avoid Loaning Free Money to Uncle Sam

CAUTION

Do not take this advice if you do not have the self-discipline to make the deposits to a money market account on each payday. (Automate it, if possible, by a payroll deduction or a charge to your checking account.) If you don't have the cash to ante up on April 15, it could cost you big bucks in penalties and interest.

Also, if your income was over $75,000 ($150,000 for married people filing jointly), you need to pay 110 percent of your prior year's income through withholding or estimated tax in order to escape any penalties.

Save Money on Nuisance Insurance (Maintenance Contracts)

Calamities come in different sizes and flavors. Perhaps for you, if your refrigerator breaks down in July, the worst-case result could be the cost of a new refrigerator and replacing the ice cream that is now a messy puddle on the freezer shelf. If that happens while the refrigerator is still under its manufacturer's warranty, you shouldn't incur any expense, except for replacing the ice cream. But breakdowns usually occur right after the warranty expires. (Manufacturers are not dumb. They know approximately how long their equipment will last without repairs.)

You can usually extend the warranty by purchasing a maintenance contract, but then the question is: Should you? If a few hundred dollars would be devastating to you, perhaps making you and your family live on rice and stale bread for several weeks, maybe you should buy the maintenance contract.

If, however, the expense of repairing or replacing the refrigerator will do no more than dig a hole in your savings account, you may be better off without the maintenance contract. In fact, with a little planning, you would probably not have to dig any hole in your savings plan. Try the following procedure.

When you purchase a product on which a maintenance contract is available, obtain the price of the contract but decline it. When you return home, write a check for the cost of the contract, payable to *yourself*, and deposit it in a special interest-bearing bank account you have set up for this purpose. Every year, as the anniversary of your purchase rolls around, buy another maintenance contract from yourself. Do this for every appliance and other piece of equipment you purchase. Then, when an out-of-warranty item needs repair, pay for the repair from that maintenance account. Unless you live under a ladder with 13 black cats for companions, you should never exhaust the maintenance account.

Do not replace the appliance by buying a new one with money in that account. That would wipe out your maintenance funds.

This should work for you. The people who offer you maintenance contracts expect to make a profit. Why not keep the profit yourself?

Figure 1.6 is an example of a form you can use to keep track of your obligations to yourself for maintenance. In this example, you would transfer $55 to your maintenance account in January, $30 in February, and so on. Just as would happen if you actually bought the maintenance contracts, in some months there would be a heavier expense for these expensive insurance contracts than in other months. However, with this do-it-yourself plan, you can overcome that. In this example, the total of all the maintenance contracts is $535. Divide that by 12 months, and you arrive at a figure of $45. Make that transfer every month, and you should come out in the same place—some extra money in the bank.

Equip	Jan	Feb	Mar	Apr	May	June	July	Aug	Sept	Oct	Nov	Dec
VCR				50								
Mower						80						
TV	55											
A/C						100						
Furnace									100			
Frig					70							
Vac											20	
D/W		30										
Washr										30		
TOTAL	55	30	0	50	70	180	0	0	100	30	20	0

Figure 1.6 Provide Your Own Maintenance Contracts

When a Maintenance Contract May Be Wise

Sometimes equipment will work haphazardly at home but behave perfectly at the repair shop. If you buy new equipment and find this to be the case, determine if the manufacturer offers a maintenance contract that extends the warranty. For this temperamental equipment, it may be smart to buy the contract and let the manufacturer stand the risk of frequent repairs.

Where to Buy a Maintenance Contract

You may find there are two sources for maintenance contracts:

1. The dealer from whom you buy the equipment (this is most likely to be offered by the mass merchandisers).
2. The manufacturer.

Be wary of the offer by the dealer or retailer. The dealer usually offers a maintenance contract at the time you buy the equipment, citing the scary hourly repair rates you face if you don't have a contract. However, most equipment comes with a manufacturer's warranty, so the dealer's contract provides double coverage during the warranty period. And that double coverage is of no benefit to you.

CAUTION

Insist that you be given a copy of the warranty before you purchase the dealer's maintenance contract. Don't buy any contract that duplicates the coverage provided by the manufacturer's warranty.

Before the end of the warranty, many manufacturers will send you an invitation to send in some money for an extended warranty. If at that time you also have the option of buying the dealer's coverage, compare not only the price but the following considerations:

- Will the repairs be made at your home or office, or will you have to lug the equipment to the repair shop?
- Will you have to package up the equipment and send it off to East Overshoe, incurring shipping charges and probably a long wait?
- What is covered? Just parts, or parts and labor?

After you have considered those questions and the price, reread this section. Do you really need coverage from anyone except yourself?

Save Money on Big-ticket Insurance

The fact that someone can afford to buy a $400 television set should indicate that they could cover the $150 repair without too much strain. That does not apply to large (in price) items. The fact that you qualify for the mortgage on a $150,000 house does not mean you could easily pay to rebuild it if it burns down or washes away, so insurance is a must for buildings, vehicles, boats, airplanes, and similar assets.

You can generally save some money on insurance by building your home next to a fire hydrant, installing a burglar alarm, having air bags in your car, and having a claims-free record of your boat insurance. But the significant savings come in much the same way as I recommended on maintenance contracts—cover, or self-insure, the small risks.

Example: You buy a new Lookalike 8 automobile for $20,000 and purchase insurance that will pay you for repair or replacement of the vehicle in the event of collision, fire, or theft. You can buy a policy that would buy you a new headlight if a rock from a dump truck hit the lens and broke it. Alternatively, you could buy a policy with a deductible of, say, $500. That means you would have to pay for replacing the headlight yourself. If you absentmindedly stopped in front of a rolling steamroller and your car was crushed (your fault), and your car just before the crushing was worth $15,000, the insurance company would pay you $14,500. You would pay the other $500, because that was the amount of your deductible.

You would buy this deductible insurance policy instead of full coverage, because the policy would cost you less money and you could reduce the price of the policy even further by buying a policy with an even higher deductible. In other words, take the risk for losses that you can financially survive, so that *you* make the profit rather than the insurance company.

EXPERT ADVICE

Treat this deductible just as I suggested for maintenance contracts: Find out what the difference is between the premium for full (or "first-dollar") coverage and the premium for the coverage with the high deductible. Pay yourself that much, preferably into a special account for the purpose, each time you send a check to the insurance company.

If there is little reduction in the insurance premium for a high deductible, choose the full coverage. However, that is unlikely to happen. It costs an insurance company almost as much in administrative expense to handle a claim for $50 as it does for $5,000, and covering the administrative expense is a significant part of the premium. Therefore, if the insurance company doesn't have to fool with your $50 claims, they can lower the price of the policy, charging you mainly for the risk, not for the claims adjusters and other employees who become involved in every claim.

More Ways to Save Dollars

There are other ways to keep some of your money for yourself. What this chapter should do is provoke some ideas about other savings areas and give you some guidance on computing the savings and cost-effectiveness of shopping. There are also more ideas later in this book. The more significant ones are the following:

- How to cut the cost of financing your purchases. Keeping a sharp pencil when it comes to interest rates and lenders' terms can save many dollars. That's covered in the next chapter, except for real estate mortgages, which are included in Chapter 6.
- Be a miserly consumer in the areas of life and medical insurance and similar products and services. How to do that is in Chapters 3 and 4.

2

More Places Where You Can Find Money

INCLUDES

- How to win in the financing games retail stores play

- How to avoid the snare of add-on fees by banks and finance companies

- Why home equity loans are the preferred way to borrow, but watch the rules

- When and how you should lease rather than buy

- How to handle the biggest factor in financial planning—you!

- Retail stores and other vendors often advertise no-interest or low-interest financing as a means of bringing you in. You can take advantage of those initial terms if you refuse to be "rolled over" into high-interest, high-fee financing *(p. 28)*

- Revolving charge accounts are little more than credit cards that are limited to one retailer. The credit card rules in Chapter 1 apply *(p. 29)*

- Avoid consumer loans from banks and finance companies if you can. At least, avoid the restructuring of loans that enable you to add on more debt. That restructuring comes with additional fees. *(p. 29)*

- If you have equity in your residence, use it for borrowing, preferably as collateral for a line of credit. The interest is usually lower, and there may be some income tax breaks. Even so, borrow only when it makes economic sense. *(p. 29)*

- Leasing, as in the acquisition of a new automobile, can sound attractive, but it comes with several traps. If you must trade up to a new car every two or three years, it may make sense to lease. If you put high mileage on your car or keep it until the wheels fall off, don't lease but buy the car. (Use cash or your home equity line of credit for this purchase.) *(p. 32)*

- You don't have to live like a sequestered monk in order to keep some of your money. Set up some simple controls on your spending and follow them to the letter. *(p. 38)*

The advice never to borrow has great merit in most situations, but in our modern economic society, confounded by perplexing tax laws, there are exceptions—home mortgages, for instance. In this chapter we look at what justifies borrowing and at how to determine the best and cheapest method of financing.

Then we end these two chapters, devoted to squeezing more money out of your income, by putting on a tattered psychologist's hat. These cash-scrimping ideas do you no good unless you use them. To help you make sure you do implement these ideas, we offer some self-motivation ideas.

Spend Less to Finance Your Purchases

Generally, the human race is composed of individuals imbued with inconsistencies. We will spend hours haggling over the best trade-in allowance for our jalopy when we buy a new Super V12 automobile and then immediately sign the first financing document the dealer puts before us. We'll shop three discount stores to find the best price on a 72-inch television set and then add the charge to a credit card that charges 22 percent interest.

The obvious advice: Shop and compare financing with as much zeal as you had when shopping for the item. What follows are explanations of and suggestions regarding some finance plans you may find offered.

Credit Cards

As covered in Chapter 1, credit cards are a convenience and sometimes a necessity if you need to reserve a motel room or rent a car. They should *not* be considered a means of financing a purchase over several months or years.

Easy Terms from Your Friendly Retail Store

Retail merchants offer many financing plans, but they pretty much fall into two broad categories: easy-payment plans for large purchases and revolving-account plans for everyday needs.

Easy-payment Plans, Sometimes with No Initial Interest

Stores that sell furniture, appliances, and other items that carry prices of several hundred dollars often offer enticing easy-payment deals. You can easily find offers of "zero down payment and no interest for 12 months." The salespeople in the store hope you can't resist. Twelve months is a year away; you certainly can pay for the new sofa by then. They hope you won't have the money to pay for it next year, so you will then start making payments at a hefty interest rate. Then, because you are in the habit of making payments, the salespeople will suggest other furniture you can add on to your account, which will increase your payment immediately at a *high* interest rate.

EXPERT ADVICE

By all means, take advantage of the 12 months of no interest.

Example: You buy a sofa with a built-in back massager with a price tag of $1,000. You have the $1,000 available, but rather than immediately paying for the sofa, you put your purchase on the store's 12-month, no-interest plan. You keep the $1,000 in your money market account for the 12 months and then pay the $1,000 to the store before the no-interest period expires. While you kept your money invested, it earned $50, so the sofa effectively cost you $950.

You could still buy the sofa on this no-interest plan, even if you do not have the $1,000 today, *if* you have the self-discipline to make payments of $84 per month to a savings or money market account for the next 12 months. Then you would have the $1,000 to pay off the debt. (You would be doing exactly what the store manager hopes you won't do.)

If there is any possibility you might end up making payments after 12 months, forget the new sofa. Keep your old one, it's paid for. (Start putting money aside for a new sofa next year. There will still be sales and no-interest deals then.)

Revolving Charge Accounts

With few exceptions, revolving charge accounts have evolved into charge arrangements that are similar to credit cards, except that their use is limited to the issuing store. As with credit cards, read the fine print before you sign up. Is there a grace period in which you can pay the balance without incurring finance charges? What is the interest rate if you do not pay off the entire balance?

Consumer Loans from Banks and Finance Companies

You can find yourself in debt to a bank or finance company if you finance a purchase at a retail store that then sells your account to a financial institution to which you end up making your payments. Banks generally charge a little lower interest rate than finance companies do, but they are fussier about your credit record. Again, the advice is to pay attention to the interest rate and read the fine print. Like retail stores, banks and finance companies want you to add new purchases on to your loan or to renegotiate your loan so that you can reduce your payment amount or skip a payment or two. The joy to your financing source is that additional fees and recomputation of interest are involved when you restructure your loan.

EXPERT ADVICE

Do not agree to restructure a consumer loan. Negotiate a new loan for an additional purchase. If the bank won't accommodate you, apply for a new loan at a different bank.

Home Equity Financing

If you must borrow money, this is the preferable way to go for two reasons:

- You can borrow at a lower interest rate, because the bank has real estate (the equity in your home) for collateral.
- Assuming you itemize your deductions on your personal federal income tax return, your effective (real) after-tax interest rate is even lower.

CAUTION

Exception: If your need for funds is short-term—only a few months—
a higher interest rate for a consumer loan from a bank might be less
expensive than the fees involved in equity financing (unless you happen upon a deal in which the bank pays the fees).

How to Calculate Your Effective Interest Cost

Look at your 1997 income tax return and at the Appendix of this book to determine your tax percentage rate. Subtract that percentage from 100 percent, then multiply the resulting percentage by the interest rate on your tax-deductible loan. The
result is the effective after-tax interest rate that you are really paying. See Figure 2.1
for an example of this calculation.

Start with	100.00%
Subtract tax rate percentage (from the Appendix)	28.00
Resulting percentage	72.00
Multiply by interest rate on your loan	9.00
After-tax or effective interest rate	6.48%

Figure 2.1 Computation of After-tax Interest Rate When Interest Is Deductible

After-tax versus Pre-tax Interest

The old saw, "compare apples to apples, not to oranges," holds true here. If the
computations in Figure 2.1 were true for you, you might think this way:

> If my real interest expense is about 6.5 percent, I should borrow
> funds in a home equity arrangement and invest them in something that
> pays more. Perhaps that would be a well-rated corporate bond paying 8.5
> percent, so I would be earning 2 percent on the bank's money.

Sorry, that won't work. That 8.5 percent income is taxable. You have to make the same
computation as in Figure 2.1 for this income, and that result is a real interest income
rate of 6.1 percent. You would be paying 6.5 percent interest for the money and receiving only 6.1 percent interest, which is anything but a get-rich-quick scheme. There
is more on this in Chapter 7.

Watch Out for the IRS and the Limitations It Imposes

The tax rules limit the deductible interest to an amount that is the interest rate times the equity in your home. That equity is computed by subtracting the current balance of your mortgage(s) from the current fair market value of your home. In other words, if your home is worth $200,000 in today's market and your mortgage balance is $150,000, you can deduct no more than the interest on the difference of $50,000. If a bank or mortgage company is willing to lend you $60,000 as a home equity loan, you would be able to deduct only five-sixths ($50,000 ÷ $60,000) of the interest.

The tax law imposes another limit: You can deduct only the interest on the first $100,000 of a home equity loan, regardless of the amount of equity in your home. (Do not confuse this with the limit on the interest on the mortgage you incur to purchase a home. That limit is the interest on $1,000,000.)

There are some other limits on deducting home equity interest. If you are involved with single-premium life insurance, tax-exempt income, related-party transactions, at-risk rules, or straddle interests, you need to confer with your tax advisor before assuming that your home equity interest will be deductible.

The Biggest Risk in Home Equity Financing—You!

The usual structure of a home equity line of credit is in the form of a line of credit. That means you do not receive a wad of cash at the closing of the loan, but you receive a credit line against which you can draw down cash as you need it. You could, of course, receive cash up to the limit of your credit line right after you sign the papers that close the home equity financing. The bank would prefer you do that, because you pay interest (income to the bank) only on the cash you draw out.

The danger is that for a while you can feel as if you are free of financial worries. You can spend freely, knowing that there is a line of credit available to you. That is, you can ignore the suggestions in Chapter 1. But the more money you borrow, the more interest you will have to pay every month; and someday the loan must be paid back to the bank. Yes, it will be paid in full when you sell your home, but consider the alternative. If you didn't use the equity in your home as a source of funds, you would have that much more cash available, from selling your home, for your retirement.

If you do set up a home equity line of credit, make a list of those expenses for which you might use it, and then stick to the list. Put off any other uses until you have accumulated the cash out of your income. Here are some suggested uses that might be justified:

- Education (yourself or children), but don't let borrowing money take the place of obtaining financial aid grants from government and private sources. Also, if this is the only reason for home equity financing, investigate an education loan. The interest may be deductible, and such a loan would avoid fees that may be involved in the home equity loan.

- Medical expenses not covered by insurance or other medical plans.

- As a method of financing *essentials*. If your old car collapses and you have to finance a replacement at 10 percent nondeductible interest, you would be better off to use your home equity source at a lower deductible interest rate. Suggestion: Find out what the payment would be if you financed the car through the dealer. Make that same payment to your home equity loan.

The discussion of the mortgage(s) you incur in purchasing your home is in Chapter 6.

Buy or Lease? The Right Answer Can Save Significantly

Another financial decision we frequently have to make is: Should we buy or lease a piece of equipment? This question is applicable only after a wisely made decision that acquiring the equipment is justified, as discussed earlier.

Example: Leasing an Automobile

What is brought to mind by the question: Buy or lease? Automobiles, for most people. That's the field in which there are proponents of leasing who encourage buyers not to buy but to lease their new cars. These proponents are known by several appellations, all of which mean "automobile salesperson." Why do they encourage us to lease a car? Their reasons include the following:

- Automobile leasing agreements use terms and computations that confuse most of us.

- In the confusion, it is possible for the salesperson to raise the price of the car and/or charge more for the use of the dealer's money (i.e., higher interest).
- Higher prices and higher interest rates result in higher commissions for the salesperson.

When Should You Lease?

All the foregoing is not to say that you should never lease an automobile. Sometimes automobile manufacturers offer subsidized lease plans, in which the manufacturer picks up some of the interest charges involved. That allows the dealer to offer attractively priced leases. That can make it attractive for you but *only if* you fit the mold of one who should lease, and we'll describe that mold a little later.

DEFINITION

Lease: When you lease your VW or Bentley or whatever, you agree to pay the dealer a set monthly amount for a specific period. For instance, you might agree to pay $350 per month for 36 months. In exchange, the dealer provides you with a car for the 36 months, at the end of which you return the car to the dealer and, in theory, have no further obligation.

The Downside of Leasing

There are some potholes in this leasing road:

- Leasing is great until the day comes when you have to return the car to the dealer. Unless you strike another deal, you will have to walk home and walk to everywhere else you want to go!
- You will be limited as to how much mileage you can run up on the odometer without incurring extra charges. (Allowed mileage is usually 12,000 to 15,000 per year, with the extra mileage charge being 11 or 12 cents per mile.)

- If you return the car with a crinkled fender, cola stains on the upholstery, and a strange clanking noise in the engine, you will be charged for the repairs to the car.

- If you want to keep the car at the end of the lease period, you will have to buy it from the dealer, albeit at the reduced price agreed upon when the lease was signed.

- All these extra you-will-pay terms should be spelled out in the lease.

Why would you let yourself get embroiled in an arrangement like this? For these reasons:

- The payments will be less than if you financed the purchase (over the same number of months) by borrowing the *total cost* of the car.

- You return the car to the dealer at the end of the lease, which is probably about at the expiration of the warranty. Your out-of-pocket repair costs will be minimal, so long as you did not abuse the car.

- You are relieved of the hassle of trying to sell the car yourself at the end of the lease.

- At the end of this lease, you can lease another brand-new car complete with the manufacturer's warranty.

CAUTION

What I have described here is a closed-end lease. That term means that the future value of the car on the used car market is determined when the lease is signed. The dealer takes the risk that it might be worth less three years later.

An open-end lease is a similar arrangement, but you take the risk of what the car will be worth at the end of the lease. If it is worth less than expected, you will have to ante up.

For most of us, the closed-end lease lets us sleep better at night.

Lease Payments Are Lower

Why are the lease payments less than the payments would be if you financed the car? Because in a lease you are financing only the difference between the price of the new car and its value three years down the road. In regular financing of a purchase, you are financing the difference between the price of the new car and zero (assuming a zero down payment.)

Example: You negotiate the price of the car you purchase to be $16,000 and agree that in three years it will be worth $6,000. If you lease the car, the difference of $10,000 is the amount that is financed over three years, and the monthly payment for that $10,000 at 8 percent interest is $350. (You pay the additional $6,000 by returning the car at the end of three years.)

If you finance the entire $16,000 for three years at 8 percent interest, the payment is $501.38. If you pay this higher figure, you keep the car after the payments cease. As an alternative, if you finance the $16,000 over five years, the payment is $324.

When, or Why, Should You Lease?

If you need to trade up to a new car every two or three years, a two- or three-year lease may be your best bet. Be careful about why you have this need. If it's for job-related appearances, leasing could well be appropriate. For instance, you lug prospects and customers around in your car.

The Good Things That Can Happen If You Don't Lease

However, if you need new cars frequently because you wear them out driving 75,000 miles a year, the extra mileage charges would kill the lease deal. If you like to trade every two or three years just to feel good, think carefully about your alternatives.

Figure 2.2 provides a comparison between continuous leasing of automobiles for 10 years and the purchase (conventional financing) of an automobile that you keep for 10 years. The computations assume that the automobile is driven 15,000 miles per year and that there is no inflation, so all leases start with the same $16,000 cost. (That's to keep it simple.) The calculations also use 8 percent interest in both the lease and finance calculations. Note that the financing alternative uses a five-year loan, so that the lease payment and the finance payment are within $25 of each other.

Assumptions:		
Cost of automobile		$16,000.00
Interest rate for financing or lease		8.00%
LEASES:		
Monthly payment	$ 350.38	
Total paid over 10 years		
(120 payments)		42,045.60
FINANCED:		
Monthly payment	324.42	
Total paid over 10 years		
(60 payments)	19,465.20	
Additional repairs	5,000.00	
Total of payments and repairs		24,465.20
Difference in total paid (total lease payments		
minus total finance payments and repairs)		$17,580.40

Figure 2.2 Leasing versus Purchasing

EXPERT ADVICE

Can you really keep a car dependable for 10 years and 150,000 miles? Check the consumer magazines. Some brands do that easily if given scheduled maintenance. (I own a 12-year-old Volvo that is about to turn over 200,000 miles. It is still dependable transportation.)

As Figure 2.2 indicates, the buy-it-and-drive-it scene saves over $17,000, even after allowing $5,000 for additional maintenance and repairs on the car. But there is more. After you pay off the automobile loan, why not continue with the monthly payment of $324 but make it to yourself? You are already used to that much coming out of your budget every month, so just change the payee to your favorite mutual fund or some other kind of investment.

Even if your investment choice is not the best and you earn only 10 percent, you will have a nest egg of $25,122, assuming you can keep the tax bite low, as covered later in this book.

EXPERT ADVICE

If you are successful in making yourself do this for the full five additional years, reward yourself by taking your payments and investment earnings for the last year (a total of $6,071) and spend it on a great vacation. You will still have over $19,000 left. Further suggestion: Buy your next car for cash and continue socking away the $324 per month.

Lease and Rental of Other Equipment

Most leasing of equipment other than automobiles is of business equipment. The decision to lease such equipment is motivated by tax and financial disclosure considerations that are beyond the scope of a personal finance book. However, you do find advertisements by stores that rent furniture and appliances to consumers. If you need a television set for a week because yours is broken and in the TV hospital, renting a replacement for a short term might make sense. (But consider doing without a television for a week—that can create seven illuminating days and save a few bucks to boot.)

Generally, you should avoid the merchants who offer to rent an appliance to you for a long period, after which you will own the refrigerator, microwave, television, or whatever. The market for this operation is the group of people who have no extra cash and no credit. The dealer continues to own the equipment until the rentals have paid for the appliance and for the cost of the dealer's money involved, and that may be at a very high rate.

If you are tempted by such an offer, find out what the true interest rate is. Obtain the price of the appliance in a discount or other competitive store. Then make a computation such as the one shown in Figure 2.3, which computes a guesstimate of the interest if you agree to a rental/purchase of a $700 refrigerator for $30 per month over 30 months.

	LINE	
Monthly rental of refrigerator	1	$ 30.00
Number of months to pay for ownership	2	30
Total cost (line 1 times line 2)	3	900.00
Cost of same model in discount store	4	700.00
Average outstanding balance (line 4 ÷ 2)	5	350.00
Cost of financing (line 3 minus line 4)	6	200.00
Monthly interest rate (line 6 ÷ line 5 ÷ line 2)	7	1.90%
Approximate annual interest rate (line 7 × 12)	8	22.80%

Figure 2.3 Computation of Interest Charge in Rental/Purchase Arrangement

The 23 percent computed in Figure 2.3 is a rough approximation you can do quickly with a pocket calculator. The more accurate rate is 21 percent. How to compute that rate is explained in the Appendix.

How to Motivate Yourself to Control Your Money

At this point, you may be saying, "This is all well and good, but it sounds as if I'll live in a straitjacket. I can buy only essentials, and much of that spending can happen only in the future. I realize I am saving for retirement, but what if I don't live that long? And I must make calculations and keep records—the fun has gone from life!"

Keep Some Fun in Your Life (Reward Yourself)

It is not necessary to deprive yourself of all pleasure. Just as you plan ahead for the essential expenditures, you should also plan ahead for a little fun. Life really should be enjoyed, and it can be enjoyed more with a little bit of planning. How? Try these steps:

1. Make a wish list of nonessentials and luxuries you would like to own or fun things to do that cost money—travel, for instance. Do not spend any money for these items—yet.

2. Determine a specific percentage of how much of your savings (from willpower and careful shopping) you will sock away in an investment account and how much you will spend on enjoying life.

3. At the end of each month, determine how much you have saved. Put the amount specified by the predetermined percentage in your investments, then pick an item from your wish list and buy it. Or accumulate that wish list money for several months in order to buy a larger luxury.

Example: After our friend Mary controlled her impulse buying, she refined her saving process this way: First, she made a list of monthly *essential* expenses, totaled it up, and subtracted that total from her net pay. (Net pay is the figure on her check after deductions for income and Social Security taxes.) Her computation, shown in Figure 2.4, indicates that she would have $600 per month left after these essential expenses. As you can see from Figure 2.4, except for talking on the telephone and watching cable television, she would be living the spartan life of a nun. However, she didn't follow that course.

Monthly net pay		$2,900
Essential expenses:		
Automobile payment	$300	
Automobile—gas, oil, maintenance	150	
Cable TV	50	
Clothing, basic and business	100	
Groceries	400	
Insurance	150	
Miscellaneous	100	
Personal items, cosmetics, etc.	50	
Rent	700	
Telephone	50	
Utilities	250	
Total essential expenses		2,300
Available for savings and nonessentials		$ 600

Figure 2.4 Calculation of Net Income and Essential Expenses for an Individual

Date	Explanation	Additions to Investment Account	Additions to Nonessential Account	Balance in Nonessential Account
1/31/98	Payday	$ 400	$ 200	$ 200
1/17/98	Dinner & show		(100)	100
2/28/98	Payday	400	200	300
3/20/98	Evening gown		(200)	100
3/28/98	Payday	333	167	267
4/10/98	Bonus	667	333	600
4/20/98	New VCR		(250)	350
4/30/98	Payday	400	200	550
5/10/98	Tax refund	1,867	933	1,483
5/20/98	Designer jeans		(110)	1,373
5/31/98	Payday	400	200	1,573
6/15/98	Detail car		(50)	1,523
6/30/98	Payday	333	167	1,690
7/10/98	Bonus	600	300	1,990
7/31/98	Payday	400	200	2,190
8/10/98	Treadmill machine		(350)	1,840
8/31/98	Payday	333	167	2,007
9/05/98	Vacation		(2,000)	7
10/10/98	Payday	933	467	474
10/31/98	Payday	400	200	674
11/30/98	Payday	400	200	874
12/20/98	Christmas shopping	_____	(500)	374
		$7,866	$ 374	

Figure 2.5 Self-motivation and Saving Plan for an Individual

What she did do was make this decision: For every $3 that she had left at the end of the month, she put $2 into her investment account and $1 into her luxury account. (She compared the fees at several banks and found one that would allow her to set up a separate "luxury" account without additional service fees.) Then, if she wanted to make a nonessential or luxury purchase, she did so only if she had sufficient funds in the luxury account.

Figure 2.5 is a record of Mary's investment account (third column) and luxury account (fourth column). The fifth column is a running balance of her luxury account. (By incorporating the balance column in this record, you could keep both the investment funds and luxury funds in one bank or brokerage account—if you can handle the tedium of detailed bookkeeping that would be involved.)

This procedure is simpler than keeping a full-blown bookkeeping system that requires you to categorize every check you write. For instance, you are stuck for a monthly expense for rent or mortgage payment. Keeping track of it won't reduce it, so just keep it in a general category of essential expenses. (Accountants and economists call them "fixed" expenses.) What you do need to control are your nonessential (buzzword is "discretionary") expenses, and this simple plan should help you do that, as well as reward yourself for controlling expenses.

Include Your 401(k) Plan in Your Planning

If you are eligible to contribute to a 401(k) plan or some other tax-deferred savings plan, you will have to modify the record in the Mary example. For the monthly net pay figure in Figure 2.4, add the deduction for the 401(k) contribution, or similar deduction, on to the net check amount for this line. Then, in Figure 2.5, list the 401(k) deduction in the investment column and make the related deposit into your luxury account. In other words, you treat the 401(k) deduction as if you had received the cash, and then you write a check for your contribution to the plan.

3

Protect Your Earning Power from Calamities

INCLUDES

- Insurance to pay the bills when you're sick or disabled. What you need and what you don't need.

- Insurance to pay the bills after you leave this life. What kind do you need and how much do you need?

- Where to find advice, facts, and figures.

FAST FORWARD

- The first priority is disability insurance. A disabled breadwinner is a bigger burden on a family than if he or she were dead. *(p. 45)*
- Don't depend on government programs. They are inadequate and often unavailable. *(p. 45)*
- Purchase disability insurance in addition to any provided by your employer (unless it's exceptional). *(p. 46)*
- Be certain that it covers illness-related as well as accident-related disabilities. *(p. 47)*
- Disability should provide income until pension benefits and Social Security kick in. *(p. 47)*
- Almost everyone needs some type of "life" insurance (actually, "early death insurance"). *(p. 51)*
- Be sure the policy states that you can continue the insurance even if you become an unattractive risk (because of illness or your activities). *(p. 53)*
- Insurance can come with investment features. That's appropriate for some people but not for all. *(p. 54)*
- Before committing to an insurance policy, seek advice from those who work for fees, not commissions. *(p. 59)*

If you have a spouse, children, and other people who depend on you to labor daily and bring home the bacon (nonfat, of course), you should be concerned about what happens if you can't work because of an accident, disease, or even your death. Let's start with the accident or sickness disability.

Who Pays the Bills If You Are Injured or Sick and Can't Work?

Probably the biggest financial disaster that can befall a family occurs when the principal breadwinner becomes disabled. This can be a bigger calamity than death. If the source of the largest part of the family income is disabled, the healthy spouse not only has the challenge of providing for the children but also for a disabled spouse. On the other hand, if the principal provider dies, the surviving spouse has fewer responsibilities, and he or she is also free to marry someone else.

The first insurance that a family should buy is disability insurance that will replace the income of one or both spouses if they should become disabled and unable to work. Yet, most people buy life insurance long before they think about disability insurance, which really is reversing priorities.

Depend on the Government? Ha!

We live in a era when the government supposedly tries to take care of our needs and wants, but does it do it? Let's take a look.

Social Security Benefits

Social Security, as it was conceived, is supposed to take care of a dependent family when a wage earner becomes disabled. Should you depend on this source of income if you carelessly stand in front of a moving steamroller? No way! Part of the federal government's budget-cutting process has been to prod the Social Security Administration to tighten up on the definition of disability. You can virtually depend on your initial claim being turned down, so you will probably have to appeal the decision, and even if you win the appeal, your first check will be months or years away—and grocery stores do not accept pending Social Security appeals in payment for meat, potatoes, and broccoli.

Workers' Compensation Benefits

If you are disabled as a result of a work-related injury, you will probably receive some benefit from your employer's workers' compensation insurance, but you will probably find the benefits to be inadequate. If you suffer disability from an accident at home or anywhere that is not related to your job, workers' compensation benefits will be zero. Also, it is extremely rare that workers' compensation would cover disability from an illness. (Try proving that your illness is job-related.)

Disability Insurance from Commercial Insurance Companies

Inasmuch as government sources probably will not supplant your income if you suffer a major disability, you will have to find this protection elsewhere—either by buying a disability policy directly from an insurance company or under your employer's plan if your employer has one.

What to Look For in an Individual Disability Insurance Policy

Unfortunately, insurance companies have had to pay more claims on disability policies than they expected, so this insurance is becoming increasingly difficult to obtain. You may be reduced to having to buy whatever is obtainable. However, if you are turned down by the first insurance company you contact, don't give up. Try others, and involve at least two or three different agents. (See "Where to Find Advice" later in this chapter.)

If you are in good health and do not have a record of disabling injuries, you still may be able to pick and choose between policies. Here is a list of what to look for:

- How long do benefits continue if you are permanently disabled? Some policies may be for as short as 24 months. If you are disabled for life, you should get coverage for life. At least, you should buy coverage that lasts until Social Security and any pension benefits kick in.
- How much is the monthly benefit amount? This will be a dollar amount, and you will find that you cannot obtain insurance for much over 60 percent of your usual income.
- Is the policy noncancelable and guaranteed renewable? That is, can the insurance company cancel the insurance or refuse to renew it at the end of a policy period if it decides to get out of the disability insurance business or if you develop a disease that may eventually disable you?
- Is the premium set at a definite rate, or is it allowed to increase only as the cost-of-living index increases? If not, the insurance company could price you out of coverage.

DEFINITION

Premium: *fancy word for price (of insurance); what you pay the insurance company periodically to keep a policy in force.*

- Does the dollar amount of benefits increase with the cost of living?
- The policy should cover disability from accidents *and* diseases. Don't buy just an accident policy. They are much cheaper because the odds of your being seriously disabled from accidents are much lower than those for being disabled from disease.
- Check on the elimination period—that is, the length of time you must be disabled before the policy starts paying benefits. The longer the elimination period, the cheaper the policy. In other words, if you have enough rainy-day savings to enable your family to survive for six months without your income, buy a policy with a six-month elimination period. (Put what you will save on monthly premiums in your rainy-day fund. You will almost assuredly come out ahead.)

- What is the policy's definition of disability? Will you be considered disabled if you cannot work in your usual occupation, or must you be unable to work in any occupation? Example: If a lawyer has a "usual occupation" clause in his or her policy, the lawyer would be covered in the event of a substantial brain disability. A lawyer who has an "any occupation" clause in the policy might have to take a job as a dishwasher or street cleaner.

- Is partial disability covered? "Partial disability" usually refers to the status of individuals who are recovering from total disability. Example: Edmund falls off his bicycle and suffers injuries that make him completely unable to work for a year, during which he receives full benefits from his insurance. During the next three months he is able to work only four hours a day. Because his policy does cover partial disability, he receives 50 percent of his benefit to cover the four hours per day he cannot work.

- Tax status: Are the premiums tax-deductible and are the benefits tax-free? There is no *deduction* for premiums unless they are provided by your employer as nontaxable fringe benefits. The *benefits* are not taxed unless the premiums are provided by the employer and not taxed. In other words, a nontaxable employer benefit may not be to your advantage. When you are disabled and living on 50 or 60 percent of your former income, a large income tax bill is the last thing you need.

See Figure 3.1 for a suggested form to use in evaluating disability insurance. Unfortunately, there are so many factors involved that it is impossible to create a meaningful formula to help you make a decision. However, this form will lay out the facts so you can make an informed judgment.

	Insurance Company 1	Insurance Company 2	Employer's Group Insurance
Benefit period	2 years	To age 65	5 years
Benefit amount (monthly)	$800	$2,000	1,500
Elimination period	6 months	3 months	3 months
Noncancelable & renewable	No	Yes	No
Limit on premium increase	No	CPI	No
Benefits increase by CPI	No	Yes	Yes
Definition of disability	Very strict	Reasonable	Strict
Usual or any occupation?	Any job	Usual occupation	Usual 2 years Any thereafter
Partial disability	No	Yes	Yes
Benefits taxable?	No	No	Yes
Monthly Premium*			

*Premium figures are omitted. There is too much variance between occupations and locations to create reasonably representative dollar figures for this example.

Figure 3.1 Comparison of Disability Income Insurance

Employer-provided Disability Insurance

If your employer makes group disability insurance available to you, it may be your best bet. Group premiums are usually less expensive, but the trade-off is probably that the insurance company or your employer could cancel the policy (for all members of the group) at any time. In evaluating your employer's disability insurance, use the same criteria as listed earlier for individual policies.

Other Sources of Disability Insurance

If you are a member of an association that offers disability insurance to its members, by all means analyze that program as you consider your employer's plan and what may be available in individual policies.

Gross salary, per month	$5,000
Subtract monthly expenses that go away if disabled:	
Income tax	$600
Social Security tax (7.65% of salary and wages)	383
Disability insurance premium	200
Commuting expense	400
Work clothes/business attire	50
Total expenses that disappear	1,633
Income needed to support family	3,368
Add continuing contributions to retirement plan	
(Disability benefits cease at age 65)	500
Total needed for the present and for retirement	$3,868

Therefore, approximately $3,900 per month would be the required benefit. However, that is 78 percent of the salary, which is a higher percentage than most insurance will cover.

Note that the Social Security tax reduces from 7.65 percent to 1.45 percent above a certain annual income level ($65,400 in 1997).

This calculation assumes that the premiums are paid with after-tax dollars. (That is, the premiums are not a deductible expense.) If the premiums were deductible, the income tax would not be a subtraction in this computation.

This also assumes that medical insurance would cover care while the individual is disabled. If there are gaps in the medical coverage, the disability insurance should be increased to cover those gaps.

Figure 3.2 Computation of Disability Insurance Needed

How Much Disability Insurance Do You Need?

The answer depends on several factors. Figure 3.2 is a worksheet that can help you decide. The computation indicates a need for about $3,900 in monthly disability benefits. That is nearly 78 percent of current income, and it is almost impossible to buy that much insurance coverage. The reason: Insurance companies do not want a lingering disability to appear more attractive than returning to work.

Some people lucky enough to work for certain employers do have a way around this limitation on benefits. At least one insurance company writes a separate disability policy that will continue contributions to a retirement plan while you are disabled, but it is sold only to employers, not to individuals. If you had that coverage, then the basic coverage needed ($3,368 in the example in Figure 3.2) would be only 67 percent of current income, and that might be possible to find. (Actually, if the company you work for offers the retirement coverage, it would most likely also offer the basic coverage.)

Who Pays the Bills If You Are Dead?

Life insurance is, in reality, "death insurance." When you buy this coverage, you are protecting your dependents against the possibility that you will die before they can support themselves. Usually, we think in terms of providing for children, but you may also need life insurance that will, upon your demise, take care of elderly or disabled parents or your spouse. So you do need some insurance unless you are single, expect to stay single, and have no relatives who might become dependent on you.

Here Is Basic, Unembellished Life Insurance

Life insurance, in its pure form, without frills, is akin to betting on the Super Bowl or the World Series or any sports contest.

Example: George is 25 years old and a nonsmoker in good health. A life insurance company will give him odds of 1,000 to one that he won't die this year. So George pays the insurance company $1. (Technically, he becomes the *insured.*) If he dies during the year, the insurance company pays $1,000. Of course, if George is dead, he isn't around to collect the $1,000. That goes to the person he designated as his *beneficiary* when he bet the $1. If George loses the bet (he hopes he will lose it), the insurance company does not pay off. Note that the insurance company keeps the $1 if George wins (dies) also, so it really pays off to the tune of only $999.

DEFINITION

Beneficiary: *The person(s) or organization(s) to whom the insurance company writes the check after you die (if you have faithfully paid your premiums).*

CAUTION

The numbers in these examples are chosen for simplicity. They are not necessarily the prices for which you can buy insurance.

Seventy years later, when George is 95 years old, he wants to make the same bet with the insurance company. Now, however, he finds that the insurance company wants him to bet $330 to its $1,000 that he will die during the year. Obviously, the insurance company wants the better odds because at age 95 George is far more likely to die within one year than he was at 25. (The $330 is a hypothetical premium. George is not likely to find an insurance company that will insure the life of a 95-year-old for any amount.)

This example portrays life insurance in its basic form, usually called *term* life insurance. The insured (George) buys one year (the term) of death benefit at the beginning of each year. Then each year, when he makes a new bet (pays his premium), his cost of insurance rises. Each year is a new deal with the insurance company, and it can refuse to take George's bet if he has become ill or injured, because those events could increase the odds that he will die during the year. Alternatively, the insurance company can now classify George as "high risk" and quote him a higher than normal bet on his part (i.e., the *insurance premium*).

Insurance companies do sell this basic type of insurance, but they prefer to sell more complex versions of life insurance. They will tell you that the reluctance to sell it is out of concern for the people they insure. There is also another motivation: This basic insurance is a commodity. If every insurance company sold nothing but this product, it would be easy for the rest of us to compare and buy the cheapest, just as one might buy a bushel of corn. Therefore, almost all insurance is sold with additional bells and whistles, some of which you should probably buy, and many of which you should probably not buy. Here are some of the more common bells and whistles:

Embellished Life Insurance

Life insurance comes with various bells, whistles, and wrappers. New frills are constantly being developed, so that the range of types of policies and the murky jargon accompanying them can create great bewilderment for those of us who do not work in the industry. There is, I believe, much validity to the charge that this is by design of the insurance marketing people. Confused customers are likely to buy more profitable products. On the other hand, there is some basis for the industry's argument: Everyone's financial needs are different, so the more wrappers there are for life insurance, the more likely it is that an insurance agent can offer a product that fits the client's need. The offset to that is that insurance companies bundle up far more than insurance in many of their wrappers, often at high profits. At any rate, some of the more common terminology, bells, and whistles deserve some description and comment.

Renewable Term Life Insurance

The addition of "renewable" means that George can renew the policy each year for a specified number of years, regardless of his health or other circumstances. If George bought his renewable policy on January 1, 1998, took up hang gliding in June, skydiving in September, and had a heart attack in November, the insurance company would still have to accept his payment of premiums and provide insurance coverage for 1999. If his policy were not renewable, the insurance company would surely tell him, "Sorry, your coverage ends on December 31, 1998, and you are finished as an insured at this company, but thank you for your past business and money."

Level-Premium Term Life Insurance

This is term insurance in which the term is for a number of years, although the premium is paid at least annually. In our first example about George, the premium increased each year with the increase in the odds that George would die during the year. A level premium levels the premium out over the number of years of the term, which might be 5, 10, or 20 years. So although George's basic term policy cost him a first-year premium (bet) of $1, the premium for his 20th year, when he will be 45, might be $2. If he buys a 20-year level-premium term policy, his premium might be $1.50 for each of the 20 years. In effect, George would overpay in the early years and underpay in the later years. Moral: Do not buy level-premium term insurance unless you are sure that you will pay the premiums and keep the policy for the full length of term. If you buy a 20-year level-premium term policy and then cancel it after five years, you will have grossly overpaid for the protection.

Convertible Term Life Insurance

The convertible feature allows you to convert the term insurance policy to whole life or other insurance product. These are discussed later in this chapter.

Note that these terms can be combined. You could have an insurance policy that is labeled, "Renewable Level-premium Convertible Term Life Insurance."

Decreasing Term Life Insurance

In this variation, the death benefit (the amount that the policy pays your heirs in the event of your death) is reduced each year. Because the amount the insurance company might have to pay goes down each year, it can charge the same premium every year. (Compare that to the basic insurance in the George example. The death benefit stays the same over the years, but the premium rises each year.) Decreasing term is often sold as "mortgage insurance" that will pay off your mortgage if you die. (Just as the principal balance on your mortgage decreases each year, the death benefit amount of the insurance can decrease also.)

Cash-value Life Insurance

Life insurance policies that provide not only a death benefit but also include a savings or investment fund are in essence comprised of two financial products:

1. A term life insurance policy.
2. An investment (savings) account.

They work together this way: If George buys a basic cash-value life insurance policy when he is 25 years old, the insurance company might charge him a premium of $2 per year for his $1,000 policy.

However, the term policy part that covers his death benefit costs only $1, as we saw earlier. What does the insurance company do with the other dollar? Pay commissions and executive salaries? Yes, with part of it. Let's assume that that part is four cents. The insurance company puts the other 96 cents into a savings account for George. In the second year, the premium for the term insurance part of this package might be $1.03. The insurance company keeps four cents for its needs, and puts the remaining 93 cents into the "George" savings account.

Now, look ahead another 24 years. George is 50 and the premium for the term insurance (the death benefit) part of this package is $3. Does the insurance company start collecting $3 or more from George? No, because it agreed, when it sold him the policy, that his premium would always be $2 per year. Remember that the investment account part of the package has been earning interest over all these years. The insurance company gets that other dollar from part of the earnings of that investment account.

The savings account part of this package is also called the "cash value," hence the name of this type of policy. If you are covered by one of these, you can borrow money from the insurance company, using the cash value of the policy as collateral.

Why Not Buy Term Insurance and Run Your Own Savings Account?

The quick answer to this question is: A lot of people do just that. If you do that, there are some advantages:

- You can make your own decision as to what sorts of investments you want to put your savings funds into. In the basic cash-value insurance policy, with a guaranteed premium charge, the insurance companies invest very conservatively in bonds and mortgages. You may be able to do much better in mutual funds, real estate, and other investments.
- You avoid various fees that the insurance company may deduct from the savings part of your policy.
- You know what you are paying for insurance and, separately, for investment management.

If you choose to do your own investing, eventually your financial history should look like this: When you start the program, the death benefit from a decreasing term policy is high and your investment fund balance is low. As time goes on, your investments increase (you hope), and therefore you need less death benefit, so that decreases over the years.

How much should you stash into an investment account to carry out this plan? First, determine how much you want to leave your family if you stand in front of a moving steamroller. Then, find out what a basic cash-value insurance policy with that much death value would cost. (Ask for a quote on a "whole life" policy.) Also get a quote on a decreasing term policy that starts out with the same death benefit amount. Subtract the second from the first and invest that difference. Also, buy the decreasing term insurance policy. What should happen is that as the death benefit of the decreasing term diminishes, your investments increase, so that you still leave your family your target amount of cash and investments.

There are some other factors to consider before taking this course to fulfill your life insurance needs:

- The earnings in the cash value portion of an insurance policy are not taxed, whereas the earnings in your invest-it-yourself account usually will be subject to income tax each year. Of course, if you put your investment account in a Roth IRA, you will shelter the earnings on the investments just as they would be sheltered in a cash-value life insurance policy.

> ### DEFINITION
>
> *New in 1998: **A Roth IRA** is a special savings and retirement account with a tremendous tax break: You never pay income tax on the earnings (interest, dividends, and capital gains) if you follow certain rules, but your contributions to this type of IRA are not deductible. The basic rules are: You must have earned income at least equal to the amount of your contribution; the annual contribution is limited to $2,000 ($4,000 for a married couple); withdrawal of earnings cannot be made until five years after opening the IRA, and withdrawals cannot be made until your are either 591/2 or disabled. Withdrawals are allowed for a first-time home purchase.*

- Do you have the self-discipline to make the contributions to the investment part of the program? While failing to make a life insurance premium payment can cause cancellation of the policy and lack of financial protection for your family, failing to make additions to your investments results only in less of an investment total than you planned to have. If you are weak in this area, you may be better off with the payment discipline imposed by an insurance company.

More Confusion: The Varieties of Cash-value Life Insurance

Most insurance companies offer even more variations.

Whole Life

This is the term that describes the basic cash-value life insurance we have already covered.

Variable Life Insurance

This policy is based on the concept of whole life, except that the cash-value portion can be invested, at your option, in common stocks. In other words, besides the protection aspect, the policy could build up a bigger kitty from which you could borrow.

Universal Life Insurance

This is similar to whole life with this exception: You can vary the amount of premium you pay. If you pay enough for a few years, the cash value will build up. If you fail to pay premiums for a few months, the insurance company can use the funds in the cash-value account to pay the premiums on the death benefit portion. If you stop your payments long enough, the cash value will be gone and the death benefit insurance will be canceled for nonpayment.

Because of this flexibility, these policies come with disclosure. That is, you should be given periodic statements as to how much of your money has gone for the death benefit (term insurance) portion of the policy, how much into the investment (cash-value) portion, and how much for fees and commissions.

Combinations of Bells, Whistles, and Wrappers

As you might expect, the marketing people at life insurance companies are constantly putting these basic types of policies into the mixing vat and scooping out new combinations. You can buy variable universal life insurance, adjustable life policies, interest-sensitive policies, and many other combination products. You can also select from a variety of payment schedules. You can buy a policy for which you will pay premiums until they cart you off to the morgue, or you can make one payment up front and be insured for life. You can elect to pay for a lifetime of protection in a few years (as in 10-year- or 20-year-pay policies). The shorter the period in which you pay premiums, the higher the premium for a given amount of insurance protection.

How Much Life Insurance Do You Need?

If you and your family are middle income with a modest estate, the primary goal of life insurance is to provide an income flow that will allow your survivors to live in the lifestyle to which they are accustomed. Figure 3.3 illustrates how this decision might be made for a specific circumstance, and it comes up with a need for $700,000 of insurance for a middle-income family. Note that these figures are round numbers to demonstrate the process. You should modify this calculation to fit your own situation.

Life insurance companies have computer programs, which your agent can access, to evaluate your situation and recommend the insurance products you should sign up for. Inasmuch as these recommendations are by the insurance company, you can expect them to be weighted in favor of the life insurance cash value as opposed to other investments. In other words, get the recommendation from your insurance agent, but pass it by an objective advisor.

Your annual cash income from your job		$50,000
Add employee benefits:		
Health insurance	$5,000	
Additional child care	2,000	
Additional life insurance, surviving spouse	1,000	
Total benefits		8,000
Total income		58,000
Subtract:		
Social Security benefits for children	3,000	
Social Security tax you no longer pay	3,825	
Contributions to pension plan/401(k)	5,000	
Job-related expenses (commuting, clothes)	4,000	
Eliminate expense of one of two automobiles	2,000	
Eliminate one automobile's loan payments	4,000	
Your food consumption	1,000	
		22,825
Income needed by surviving family		$35,175
Investment funds needed by surviving family to generate needed income at 5 percent earning rate (Divide needed income by return rate)		$703,500

Figure 3.3 How Much Life Insurance Do You Need?

CAUTION

If your estate is more than the specific minimum amount allowed by law, you should start to get concerned about paying estate taxes. That minimum amount is currently being raised by a new schedule in the tax law that increases it from $625,000 in 1998 to $1,000,000 in 2006.

The Bottom Line—What Should You Do About Life Insurance?

There is no magic formula that everyone can use for a guide to purchasing insurance, but these comments should be helpful:

Remember that the primary product of life insurance companies is death benefit insurance. Compare their other products with what is available in the general marketplace.

- If you are young, with low income and large family responsibilities, buy only the protection of term life insurance. The only bell or whistle you should pay for is the renewable feature, which will let you keep your family protected even if your health fails.

- If you are older and can set aside investment money, take a look at universal life insurance that also has a variable investment feature. Note that I said "look." Don't buy the first policy that is presented to you, and don't get hoodwinked into thinking you have to use an insurance policy for investment. Yes, there is tax shelter there, but there is also tax shelter in your 401(k) plan, conventional IRAs, Roth IRAs, and, if you're self-employed, Keogh and SEP plans.

- If you have clawed your way into the "wealthy bracket," be aware that various insurance products, in combination with other estate planning vehicles, can reduce income and estate taxes.

Where to Find Advice

EXPERT ADVICE

If you buy through an insurance agent, pick one as you would a lawyer or accountant. That is, seek referrals from friends and associates. Look for an agent who puts your interest first, rather than turning on a hard sell for products that probably have the highest commission rates. If you choose an agent who represents only one company, talk to more agents who represent other companies.

EXPERT ADVICE *(CONTINUED)*

Then, before you sign up for a long commitment to an insurance product, run your decision by a knowledgeable professional who can point out traps and needless expenses you may have overlooked. Who would that be? Many financial planners and accountants could be of some help, but one who specializes in insurance would be better. For help in locating such a planner, call the Life Insurance Advisers Association at 800-521-4578 or try Fee for Service at 800-874-5662.

CAUTION

Sometimes a life insurance agent who is compensated by commissions will masquerade as a fee-only advisor. If you find a fee-only advisor pushing you to purchase a whole life policy (big premiums and big cash value), be suspicious.

You can expect to pay from $150 to $250 per hour for a legitimate fee-only advisor. If you are buying insurance that has an investment feature, the cost of the advisor could be well worth the price.

If a fee-only advisor is out of your reach, there are at least two insurance companies that sell low-load insurance. That is, they do not sell through agents, so most of the substantial commission goes in your pocket. Before you buy elsewhere, get their quotes. Call USAA Life Insurance Company at 800-531-8000 or Veritas at 800-552-3553.

Just because an insurance company has been in business for a zillion years does not mean it can provide you with the best insurance. Look for a highly rated company. Several companies rate insurance companies for their financial strength. The best known is A. M. Best Company, which rates companies from the top of "A++" to the bottom of "F" (insurance companies in liquidation). Some insurance experts suggest buying only from companies rated "A" or better, but A. M. Best suggests that ratings of B+ or better are "secure." If you have access to the Internet, you can find a full description of A. M. Best's ratings at "www.ambest.com/guide.html". You can obtain limited information about the ratings of individual insurance companies at "www.ambest.com/resource/insdir.html". There are links to various other insurance information at "http://insweb.com/".

There are other insurance rating companies: Moody's, Standard & Poor's, Duff & Phelps, and Weiss. You can find information about them in most large libraries.

If your need is for term insurance only, don't overlook insurance that you may be able to purchase through your employer or a club or association to which you belong. These group policies often offer cheaper rates than you can find as an individual.

In a Few Words: Life Insurance and Disability Insurance

Most of us work because we have responsibilities. A major risk of life is that we will not be able to meet those responsibilities because of accident, illness, or death before we have reached old age and have outlived our responsibilities.

These risks can be reduced by careful purchase of insurance. For starters, buy just the basic *insurance* coverage you need as soon as possible. (Tomorrow may be the day you carelessly stand in front of that moving steamroller.)

Buy insurance that covers most eventualities. Don't buy insurance that limits the payoff according to *how* you became disabled or dead. (An example of such a limitation would be that you must become disabled by accident, not sickness, to collect.)

4

Protect Your Health— Keep Your Access to Medical Care

INCLUDES

- What kind of health insurance should you have?

- What kind of insurance can you buy?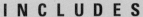

- What do the complicated buzz words mean?

- What is an HMO?

- Should you buy insurance or join an HMO?

- How can you keep your insurance in effect if you leave your job or change jobs?

- Medicare: We will all need it some-day—will it still be around?

- What are Medicare HMOs?

- How will you pay for your old age in a nursing home?

63

- Take advantage of any and all medical insurance your employer provides, even if you have to pay part of the cost. Fill in the gaps with a major medical policy. Avoid insurance that is limited to accident-related treatment only or to specific diseases (such as cancer insurance). *(p. 68)*

- If your employer's plan is an HMO, make the best of it. If you have a choice, tread carefully before you join an HMO. Read the contract carefully *before* you sign up. *(p. 68)*

- If you leave your employer, follow the continuation-of-benefit (COBRA) rules and pay the premiums so that you stay covered. This is even more important if you have pre-existing health problems. *(p. 71)*

- If your new employer provides medical benefits, follow the rules so that your coverage is continuous, even for pre-existing conditions. *(p. 71)*

- It is to be hoped that some type of government-sponsored medical plan for the elderly (Medicare) will always be around, but it won't, and it doesn't cover all the medical expenses you will have as you grow older. Buy supplemental ("medigap") insurance on the day you turn 65. If you do that, you will be covered for whatever ailments you already have. *(p. 72)*

- Like regular HMOs, Medicare HMOs are still in the growing-pains stage. Avoid them for now unless you absolutely cannot afford supplemental insurance. *(p. 73)*

- The government will pay for the years you may spend in a nursing home at the end of your life, but the plan will make you a pauper. If you want to leave something to your kids, buy long-term care insurance or become so wealthy that the $50,000 per year for nursing home care is pocket change. *(p. 73)*

As we are all aware, medical insurance and other medical service plans are in a state of flux, with costs of some medical services soaring out of sight. Whose fault is that? Probably our own, for most of us want the longer and healthier lives that modern medicine can provide. The technology and services of CAT scans, open-heart surgery, organ replacement, bone reconstruction, and other medical miracles do not come cheap. While we as a nation debate about the best way to pay for these services, each of us has to worry about today. Tomorrow may be the day we catch a serious disease or stand in front of a moving steamroller!

What Is the Best Kind of Medical Insurance?

This was a valid question 15 years ago but not now. Today, the questions are, "What kind of insurance can I get?" and "What can I afford?"

What Kind of Insurance Can I Get?

For most of us, the answer is dictated by the question, "How much can I afford?" If your employer offers medical coverage, he or she is probably paying at least part of the cost, so it makes sense to elect coverage under that plan.

Those who are self-employed or work for small companies that do not provide medical coverage have to foot the bill for medical care themselves, and that can be expensive. The descriptions of medical plans and the buzz words involved that follow are mainly for this latter group. However, it should also interest employees who are covered under an employer's plan. They should know just what their company is buying for them.

Your Doctor and Hospital Bill the Insurance Company

This is the conventional insurance that has existed for decades and now is referred to as "fee for service." You pay (or your employer pays) the insurance company a monthly *premium*. When you incur a medical bill, the insurance company pays it, or pays some of it.

However, the insurance company may not pay all of it. Even though you have faithfully paid the premiums, you may still have to cough up for the following:

Annual Deductible Amount

Every year, you have to pay the first $100, $200, $1,000, or some other specified amount of medical expense before the insurance company pays a penny.

Coinsurance

After you have paid your deductible amount, the insurance company may pay only some percentage of the bill.

Excess Charges

If your doctor or hospital bills are for more than the amount your insurance company believes to be reasonable, you pay the difference between the bill and what the insurance company pays.

Example: Pat has a pain in his tummy and checks in with his doctor. She diagnoses his symptoms as possible appendicitis and sends him to the hospital, where a surgeon fixes his problem. The total bill from the doctors, hospital, and laboratory is $12,000. Even though Pat has medical insurance, he still must pay a hefty 37 percent of the total medical bill, as shown in Figure 4.1.

Total hospital and doctor bills	$12,000
Subtract what the insurance company fee schedule allows	
for this procedure	10,000
Excess charges that Pat must pay	$ 2,000
Allowable charges, per insurance company fee schedule	$10,000
Subtract deductible amount that Pat must pay	500
Remaining amount subject to co-payment	9,500
Subtract: insurance company pays 80% of $9,500	7,600
Pat's co-payment (20%)	$ 1,900
Summary:	
Total Pat pays ($2,000 + $500 + $1,900)	4,400
Insurance company pays	7,600
Total medical expense	$12,000

Figure 4.1 Health Insurance Pays and It Doesn't Pay

If Pat buys his own insurance, he should look for a policy with a couple of enhancements, as follows:

- If the doctors and the hospital agree to participate with the insurance plan, they are limited to billing only as much as the insurance company allows. Conventional Blue Cross is an example of this concept.

- The policy should have an upper limit on the co-insurance. That is, this policy would be more appropriate for most people if the co-insurance were effective on only the first $5,000. Thereafter, the insurance company would pay 100 percent of the charges.

If these provisions had been in the insurance that Pat purchased, his share of the cost of his operation would have been only $1,200. (That's the $200 deductible and the $1,000 that is 20 percent of $5,000.)

Naturally, if the insurance company is going to pay all the expenses above $5,000, it will charge more for the insurance. That may be prohibitive for Pat, who is already paying a small fortune for this insurance. What can he do?

If he exchanged his policy for one with a much higher deductible, say $2,000, the policy would cost less. (The insurance company charges less for high-deductible insurance because it saves the administrative expense of handling a lot of small claims.)

Moral: Worry about the high end of your health coverage, not the low end. Financially, most people will survive $50 office visits or having to borrow $2,000 to cover a large deductible, but most people will not survive the 20 percent co-payment on a $500,000 bill for some high-tech medicine.

Examine your policy for upper limits on medical expense. If they're less than $1,000,000, look into purchasing a major medical policy that covers medical expense above the limits of your basic policy.

Coverage from Your Employer

Employers are not in business to provide charity to their employees. Medical insurance is expensive, so to keep fringe benefit expenses within reason, your employer may buy medical insurance with some gaps. The maximum benefit may be only $100,000 or so, the deductible may be high, and the co-payment unlimited. If this is your situation, consider buying a major medical insurance policy that picks up where your employer's insurance leaves you uncovered.

Moral: Study the information you receive from your employer about medical coverage. If there are several gaps or a low limit on benefits, try to find a major medical policy that will pay off in the event of a major medical catastrophe.

Health Maintenance Organizations (HMOs)—Probably Here to Stay

These recent arrivals on the medical scene have been around for only a few years, and they are still subject to growing pains. They claim they can provide medical care for less than the traditional fee-for-service practice of medicine and traditional insurance coverage. Although they vary somewhat in operation, the basic concept is as follows:

How an HMO Operates

- An HMO collects money every month from you (or your employer) and many other people who wish to be covered for future medical expenses.

- It enlists doctors, hospitals, laboratories, and other medical facilities to join its plan.

- When these medical providers join, they agree to accept payment for services according to a fee schedule developed by the HMO.

- When viruses and other mean things make you sick, or when you are run over by that steamroller, you naturally want some medical care and advice. To obtain that, you have to go to doctors and medical facilities that are members of the HMO. If you go elsewhere, you will have to pay for the services out of your own pocket, and that can be *very* expensive.

- In order to use the services of the HMO's doctors and hospitals, you have to select a "gatekeeper." That individual is a primary care physician. You can obtain services from specialists, hospitals, clinics, pharmacies, et cetera only with that physician's blessing and permission. (We used to call these gatekeepers "family doctors.")

- You receive all the services without paying any significant fees yourself. (Many HMOs charge a token fee of about $10 for an office visit to a doctor. That reduces the frequency of visits by hypochondriacs and strange people who enjoy sitting in medical waiting rooms.)

The Upside of HMOs

- Because of the buying clout of an HMO, it can buy medical services cheaper than you can as an individual.

- As long as you pay the monthly charge, you will receive medical services with little or no additional cost.

The Downside of HMOs

- If the gatekeeper function were left to the professional discretion of a doctor, it would work well. However, in an effort to cut costs, HMOs also impose an administrative gate that is administered by someone with minimal, if any, medical training but who can deny critically needed services. That is, you can die because some HMO bureaucrat says you do not need an operation or some expensive treatment.

- HMOs do not cover every medical problem, and they play down what they don't cover. One Florida HMO refuses to disclose what it doesn't cover (the "exclusions") until *after* you have joined its program. (Did you ever buy a pair of shoes without trying them on?) The problem with that scene is that by the time you know what isn't covered, you have probably canceled your existing health insurance.

- When HMOs start up and are rapidly expanding their client bases, the cash rolls in and they can take care of their members. However, as they mature and the cash flow from new members slows down, they may be hard pressed for the cash with which to pay for the services you need. The HMOs also need very sophisticated computer programs to know where they stand. If disaster strikes the computers, the whole operation is in trouble. At this writing, at least two large HMOs have these problems.

Which Should You Buy—HMO or Conventional Health Insurance?

If your employer provides medical coverage, your decision is pretty much made for you. If you have to buy your own medical coverage and have conventional medical insurance now, consider the following factors before you make a change.

- Do you have a pre-existing medical problem? If you have high blood pressure, diabetes, or other serious problems, you should stay with your present insurer. If you found a new plan that would accept you, it probably would not cover your present problems.

- If you want to try an HMO, read the contract carefully. Remember that you may find it difficult to switch back to conventional insurance coverage. If the HMO will not let you read the contract until after you have signed up, do not join that HMO.

What to Do If You Cannot Find Insurance or HMO Coverage Because You Have a Medical Problem

About the only route open to you is to find a job with a large company that covers its employees with a group plan that has to accept all employees as members, regardless of their health. The plan will probably exclude treatment for your pre-existing medical problem for 12 months, but after that time your problem will be covered. Then, if you change jobs, you should be able to take your full coverage with you. (See the next section.)

How to Handle Health Insurance When You Change Employers

If you change from one employer to another, both of whom provide medical insurance, you do not have to start over again on a waiting period for a pre-existing condition.

Example: When Wanda goes to work for Slavedriver, Inc., she immediately becomes covered under that company's medical plan. However, the plan excludes her from coverage for her pre-existing medical problem for the maximum the law allows, which for her is 12 months. She works at Slavedriver for seven months, quits, and then finds a new job at Easygoing, Inc. Easygoing also has a medical plan, but because of the Kasselbaum–Kennedy Law, its plan can exclude coverage for Wanda's problem for only the remainder of the 12-month waiting period (five months).

How to Handle Health Insurance If You Quit Your Job

If you leave covered employment and go to work for an employer who offers no health coverage, or if you become unemployed, you may be able to purchase an individual health insurance policy and avoid another pre-existing condition waiting period if:

- You have been covered for at least 18 months, and your last coverage was in a group plan.
- You continued the group policy you were in at your last employer by paying the premiums yourself for the continuation of benefits for as long as allowed under the continuation-of-benefits law.
- You apply for an individual policy within 62 days of the date that your continuation-of-benefits coverage expired.

EXPERT ADVICE

Consumer Reports Magazine has several analytical articles and details on medical insurance and HMO offerings. It's available in most libraries and online on CompuServe at GO CONSUMER REPORTS or on the internet at www.consumerreports.org.

Medicare (for Those 65 and Over)

This part isn't just for old folks. All who expect to retire some day need this information for their planning.

In theory, you paid for this government-administered health insurance as part of the Social Security tax you paid while you were working. In actuality, the government spent that tax money as soon as you paid it. Now it has to spend the money it collects from younger people to pay for medical services to the chronologically disadvantaged. How will the government resolve this dilemma? Who knows? But as long as the program exists, you might as well take advantage of it if you are old enough.

How Do You Sign Up?

When you are approaching your 65th birthday, the government will suggest that you sign up for Parts A and B of Medicare. Part A, which covers hospital care, is completely paid for by the government, so every eligible person is covered. Part B, which covers bills from your doctors, is optional. However, because it costs only $43.80 per month, it is a bargain. Elect coverage B. The $43.80 is deducted from your Social Security check every month, so you won't miss it.

Do You Need Supplemental Insurance?

In a word, Yes. Medicare, Parts A and B, does not cover all expenses. You have to pay part of many of the expenses (co-insurance and deductibles), and some of the benefits do not provide coverage beyond a short time. A major illness or injury can still reduce your bank account and all your other assets to zero.

Years ago, there were hundreds of Medicare supplemental insurance policies, all with varying coverage. Because some of these plans appeared too confusing, particularly to elderly people, the federal government decreed that only 10 standard plans could be offered by insurance companies. So your main choice is among the plans, and your secondary priority is to choose a company with a reputation for promptly paying benefits.

Be sure you apply for this "Medigap" insurance in the three months before you turn 65 or within six months after turning 65. During that period, the insurance company must accept you regardless of your health. Thereafter, it can exclude anyone with a health problem.

What About Medicare HMOs?

The earlier comments about HMOs apply. Generally, as long as you are visiting your primary care physician for life's little problems such as flu, colds, broken bones, and so on, you will find you are well covered, and you won't need to spend the $75 to $150 per month that supplemental insurance will cost you if you stay with the conventional Medicare.

However, when you need specialists and expensive medical treatments, you may find that these are denied to you by administrative personnel without medical training and qualifications. Also, as in regular HMOs, your choice of doctors is limited.

Recommendation: Hold off on the HMO idea until more bugs are worked or legislated out of the current HMO system.

Long-term Care Insurance

For most of us, contemplating the prospect of needing long-term care rates right up there with death as something we would rather not think about. Yet life expectancy is increasing, and many of us will live into our 90s, and if you do that, the prospect of needing long-term care is real.

Rely on the Government?

Medicare covers very little in the way of long-term care, as in a nursing home. Specifically, it covers a large share of the cost for 100 days, then nothing. Yet the average stay of an elderly person in a nursing home is four years.

If you get any more help from the government, it comes through the Medicaid program. Please note the difference between Medicare and Medicaid.

DEFINITION

Medicare *is part of the federal Social Security program. It covers all individuals 65 and over who have made sufficient contributions to the Social Security system. There is no "means" test. In other words, it covers the poor, millionaires, and everyone in between (as long as they are eligible for Social Security).*

Medicaid *is a federal and state program of health care for people (generally, children and the disabled) of any age who find themselves in poverty with no insurance or other medical plan coverage. So it does cover elderly people in nursing homes provided they have few assets and little income.*

Are You Eligible for Medicaid?

If you are comfortably retired on a moderate income with a few assets, you would not be eligible for Medicaid as soon as Medicare stopped paying, but you soon would become eligible. Because lengthy nursing home stays now cost $3,000 to $4,000 per month, you would have to sell your stocks, bonds, certificates of deposit, art, and your classic car in order to pay the bill. It won't take long to run out; then you'll be eligible for Medicaid.

CAUTION

You've probably heard that you can use a maneuver to hasten this arrival at the poverty level by giving away your money and investments to your children before you enter the nursing home. If you did it over three years before you entered, it would work. Now, however, Congress has passed a law that makes it a crime to transfer assets in order to be eligible for Medicaid in a nursing home. Seek legal advice before you try this maneuver.

5

Emergency Money and Savings for Short-term Needs

- How to compute how much you need in emergency funds
- Where to keep your emergency funds

- Emergencies crop up for many reasons: accidents, sickness, fires, floods, and many others. Even if the cost of some of these disasters is covered by insurance, you can still have a need for emergency money until the insurance company coughs up the funds—perhaps weeks later. *(p. 77)*

- Consider an open credit line as funds for emergency expenses for which you will be reimbursed. Otherwise, try to have enough to cover your needs in an emergency fund. *(p. 79)*

- Try not to guess at your emergency needs, or use a rule of thumb. Everyone's situation is different. Make some calculations as to what *your* needs are. *(p. 80)*

- Keep your emergency fund where it is safe, not only from theft and fire, but from fluctuations in its value. You want to be able to put your hands on all of your money when you need it. *(p. 80)*

- Generally, banks and credit unions offer the best of both types of protection, but watch out for bank fees. Shop for economical bank services just as hard as you shop for cheaper gasoline. *(p. 81)*

- Don't let the bank win by borrowing high and earning low. Pay off high-interest credit cards first. *(p. 81)*

Emergencies? We Have Insurance

Yes, it's easy to rationalize. You spend what you can squeeze out of your too-small paycheck for insurance. That should take care of the unexpected bills because Junior flew over his handlebars or the tornado took your roof off. But what about the quick trip for a hospital visit to rich Aunt Emma, who cracked up in her hang glider? What insurance will buy those airplane tickets? What if your employer suddenly decides to downsize, and you're one of the chosen downsizees?

So you do need a stash of cash on which you can lay your hands quickly. That raises two basic questions:

- How much do you need?
- Where do you keep it?

What follows is a discussion of each of these questions.

How Much Should You Keep in Your Emergency Fund?

Planners will spout various rules of thumb, such as: "You need to have six months of expenses in liquid assets." I don't know where the "six months" comes from, and "liquid assets" can mean various things. (My Uncle Harry used to consume his liquid assets out of large green bottles.)

Instead of some one-size-fits-all rule, take pencil and paper in hand and write down events that might make you need cash in a hurry. Then add planned events that will create a cash need.

Possible Emergencies for Which You Should Be Financially Prepared

- Travel expense if a relative or close friend becomes critically ill or dies. If you live in Chicago and your aging parents live in Hong Kong, this item will be far higher than if they live in Springfield.

- Emergency medical care for anyone in your family who is taken ill or has an accident. For this number, look at your medical insurance. How much are the deductibles and co-payments? Will your doctor and the local hospital emergency room bill the insurance company for the care, or will they expect you to pay them and wait for your reimbursement money to come from the insurance company? If you don't know your doctor's and local hospital's policy on this, call them and find out.

- What if your automobile is damaged in an accident? Will you need resources with which to rent a temporary replacement while it is being repaired?

- What if your house burns down or is ripped apart by a tornado? Are there relatives who will take you in, or will you have to live in a motel and eat in restaurants for a few weeks? Does your homeowner's or tenant's insurance reimburse you for these expenses?

Upcoming Expenses You Know About and Anticipate

- Vacations and long weekends in which your travel can run up expenses quickly.

- Holiday gift-giving. It adds up if you have a large family and many relatives.

- Replacement of your worn-out and obsolete stuff, such as your automobile, television, VCR, and other money-grabbing "necessities."

From these lists, you can generate some figure that you should have in cash or in an investment that can be quickly turned into cash. You also may have another resource: credit. To be available for use in an emergency, credit has to be immediately available. The first choice in this category is a home equity line of credit (see Chapter 6), because the interest charges will be less. In a pinch, available credit on credit cards can be used. Do not count on what you think you can borrow on any day from good old Ralph at the bank. He may be having a bad day when you go to see him and say, "NO." Count on only credit that has already been okayed.

EXPERT ADVICE

Consider giving yourself some rules for when you should use credit for meeting emergencies and when you should have cash available for them. Here's a suggestion:

- *Use credit for those emergency expenses for which you will soon be reimbursed—by an insurance company, for example.*
- *Use your credit card to cover other emergency expenses at night when the bank is closed. Immediately send a check for the amount of your expense to your credit card issuer to avoid interest charges. (Don't go to an ATM in the dark to get any amount of money; it's too dangerous.)*
- *Use your credit for any other emergency only when you have no alternative. First, try to make payment arrangements with those you owe for the emergency services. Example: Most hospitals will, although somewhat reluctantly, set up a payment schedule for emergency charges not covered by insurance. That keeps your available credit line open in case other emergencies pop up. (It seems that they often come in bunches.)*

See Figure 5.1 for a form you can adapt to your situation and fill in to get an idea of what you need in emergency cash. Tailor the form to your situation, and fill in the "Cash and Credit" columns with your best guess as to how much money might be needed. If you do not have credit available, put everything under the "Cash" column.

The totals may surprise you. For most people, the totals will be substantially more than they have in the bank. If that is your case, do not be discouraged. Re-read Chapter 1 on how to put more dollars aside.

The figure for the "Loss of Job" line is a call that *you* have to make. The key is how long it would take you to find another job with at least the same compensation. If you are a skilled engineer, technician, or mechanic and your field is open (as are computer engineering and programming and automotive electronics at this writing), a month's salary may be enough. If you are an older middle-manager with administrative skills, you may need several months of emergency funds.

Nature of Possible/Probable Expense	Cash Required	O.K. to Use Credit
Travel for family emergencies	X	
Emergency medical care, not covered by insurance	X	
Emergency medical care, to be reimbursed by insurance		X
Car rental while your vehicle is being repaired, not covered by insurance	X	
Same car rental, covered by insurance		X
Temporary living expenses due to house damage, not covered by insurance	X	
Same living expenses, covered by insurance		X
Loss of job	X	
Vacations and excursions	X	
Holiday gift-giving	X	
Replacement of worn-out appliances, etc.	X	
Totals	$	$

Figure 5.1 Form for Computing Emergency and Saving Funds Needed

Where to Keep Your Emergency Funds

There was a time when many people kept this sort of money in their mattress or hidden in some similar place. This is true of many who lived through the depression of the 1930s when banks failed and savings accounts just disappeared. Today, through the Federal Deposit Insurance Corporation, the government guarantees that a deposit of up to $100,000 is safe unless the U.S. government fails!

So, keep your money in a bank. (Your mattress could catch on fire.) That leads to other decisions you'll need to make.

What Type of Bank Account(s) Should You Keep Your Money In?

When you keep money in a bank, you are actually loaning money to the bank. It takes your money and loans it to someone else and charges that someone else interest. Does the bank, in turn, pay interest on the money you loan it? No, on some accounts. Very little on other accounts. And the bank will most likely charge you fees for the privilege of loaning your money to it! Banks do have to make a profit in order to stay in business, so they have to pay less interest to you than they charge their loan customers. Your job is to make sure that the bank shares some of that profit with you. Bank marketing departments come up with fancy names for various accounts, but they all fall into the following four basic categories.

Checking Account

You need a checking account for convenience. Writing checks and having them delivered for 32 cents beats driving all over town to pay bills. Banks pay little or no interest on these accounts, so your goal should be to keep in a checking account only enough to cover expenses between paydays. However, banks are prone to charge substantial fees if you keep too little in a checking account. Shop several banks that are convenient, providing the following information and asking about fees. (You can do this by telephone.)

- Tell the new accounts person how much you plan to keep in your checking account, on average, and what your minimum balance is likely to be.
- Ask what the monthly maintenance fees or service charges will be.
- Ask how much more you would have to keep in the account to eliminate the fees.
- Is the no-fee status based on *average* balance or *lowest* balance during the month?
- If you are over 50, does the bank offer low- or no-fee accounts for seniors?
- If you have savings accounts or loans with the bank, do the checking account fees go away?
- Ask about ATM charges. Does the bank charge if you use its own ATM when you withdraw funds from your account at the bank?

- What are the charges if you use some other ATM to withdraw cash?
- Are you charged a fee if you deposit a check that comes back because the person who gave you the check had insufficient funds in his or her account?
- Do you get your canceled checks back with your statement? If not, what is the fee for obtaining a copy of a check in case you need to prove payment to someone?
- Is there a fee for handling electronic deposits and automatic payments from your account?
- If you have other accounts at the bank (such as a savings account), can you transfer your money from one account to another by telephone?

You may think this is a lot of concern over some minor expense connected with a checking account. However, consider what this can mean over time. If you incur a monthly service fee of $10 and use the ATM eight times at $1 per transaction, you are paying the bank $18 per month, or $216 per year. If your average balance is $1,000, you are paying the bank 22 percent of your money for letting the bank use your money. (I guess that might be called reverse interest.)

So, shop well. Of course, if you have to travel 50 miles one way to get to a bank that will provide you with no-fee checking, it may not be worth it.

Don't overlook credit unions. They also offer banking services, although they use different terminology. Their "share draft" accounts are checking accounts, and their "prime share" accounts are savings accounts, and they also make loans, often at lower rates than banks do. Some credit unions offer no-fee share draft (checking) accounts. Usually, you have to work for a certain company, or in a certain industry, or meet other requirements in order to join a credit union, but check with those in your area for their requirements. You may qualify.

Once you have set up a checking account with as little of your money as will avoid the fees, it is time to decide where else to keep your emergency funds.

Savings Accounts

Banks offer savings accounts with names such as "passbook savings" and "statement savings." They are a notch up from a mattress, because your money is safer, but that's about all. The interest rate is usually very low, so look for other places in which to keep your hard-earned dollars.

Bank Money Market Deposit Accounts

Years ago, stock and bond brokers started offering a type of mutual fund that keeps cash in various safe investments that can quickly be turned into cash. They could offer higher interest rates than banks offered on savings accounts, and the savings money started to leave banks. As a result, banks also began to offer "money market" accounts, although they are just a type of savings account. However, to be competitive, banks do pay a little higher interest on these accounts than on regular savings accounts. In a way, such accounts operate as a checking account on which the bank pays you interest. (The jargon is "interest-bearing.") However, you are generally limited to three checks a month without incurring some high fees.

Obviously, a bank money market account is an excellent place to keep the emergency funds we discussed earlier. You don't even have to go to the bank to draw out the funds—just write a check.

Certificates of Deposit

If you deposit $1,000 in a bank money market account, the bank doesn't know if you will draw it out again tomorrow or leave it there for years. Because of this uncertainty, it cannot lend as much of your $1,000 to other people as it could if it were sure you would leave the money in the bank for a certain period. The result is the *certificate of deposit* (CD), which has built-in incentives to encourage you to leave your money for a definite period. Those incentives are a higher interest rate that the bank will pay you and a penalty if you withdraw the money early.

Example: Charlie bought a one-year CD, paying 5 percent interest, for $1,000. If he leaves that money in the CD for the full year, it will be worth $1,050 at the end of the year. However, if he takes his $1,000 out by cashing in his CD after only six months, he will have earned only $25 in interest, so his CD will be worth only $1,025. Also, the bank will charge him an early withdrawal penalty, which might be six months' interest, or $25. That means his $1,000, after six months, is still just $1,000.

So, put your money in a CD if you are almost absolutely sure you won't need it until the end of the period (when the CD *matures*). If it's November and you have the money for next summer's vacation saved already, putting it in a six-month CD could make sense. Longer-term CDs usually pay a little higher interest, so they are a good place to put that emergency money you hope you will never need (for the accident, fire, etc.) If worse comes to worst, you can get at your money right away, although it will cost you some penalty.

Money Market Funds

The discussion of a bank's money market deposit account alluded to these financial entities as the products that goaded the banks into offering a competitive product. The funds are essentially a mutual fund that invests only in IOUs from the federal government and large, stable corporations. (Mutual funds in general are covered in Chapter 9.) Generally, a broker's money market funds will appear to act just as a bank's money market deposit account does. That is, if you put $100 in the fund, you generally will be able to draw out $100 plus interest. These funds are available at most investment brokerage offices, and they compare with the money market accounts at commercial banks, as shown in Figure 5.2.

Feature	Money Market Deposit Accounts (Banks)	Money Market Funds
Interest earned	Determined by bank's management	Determined by marketplace
Withdrawals	Usually 3 checks per month	Unlimited
Government guaranteed	Up to $100,000 of your money is guaranteed by the Federal Deposit Insurance Corporation	Investment in fund not guaranteed but Securities Investor Protection Corporation insures you against insolvency of brokerage firm
Taxation of interest income	Taxable	Both taxable and nontaxable funds are available (Nontaxable funds pay lower interest rate)

Figure 5.2 Comparison of Bank Money Market Deposit Account to Money Market Fund

Why consider keeping your emergency money in a money market mutual fund?

- It may earn interest at a higher rate than a bank's money market fund.
- Some money market funds pay tax-free interest. That's because the funds invest in IOUs sold by state and municipal governments, and the interest on those is not subject to federal income tax.
- If you invest in stocks and bonds, the brokerage firm can take care of receiving your dividends and interest and immediately placing that money in your money market fund.

Earn 18 Percent on Your Money with No Risk

Let's say you have read this far, so you dutifully start dumping cash into a money market account at your bank, and it pays you 5 percent interest per year. While you are saving in this way, taking money out of your paycheck, you make the minimum payment on your credit card, because that is all you can spare after making the savings payment. If you do this, and the bank where you have your account is also your credit card issuer, the bank will love you. In essence, it is borrowing money from you for 5 percent interest and lending it back to you at 18 percent (or whatever rate it is charging on your credit card debt).

Don't let the bank win so easily. Do this instead. Pay off your credit card debt before adding to your savings. That won't reduce your cash available for emergencies, because as you pay off your credit card debt, you have more of your plastic card credit available for emergencies. (It's preferable, of course, to have more in interest-earning savings and not have to use available credit.)

Figure 5.3 provides an example of this concept. Pauline comes out $533 ahead by paying off her credit card balance before building up her savings because, by paying off the credit card, she is earning 18 percent on her money instead of 5 percent in a money market or some other savings account. In effect, she is earning 18 percent on her money with no risk, and it's hard to find an investment like that.

Pauline had maxed out her credit card. (She had spent up to the maximum credit limit of $10,000.) Now, after having read this book, she finds she can manage to squeeze $1,000 per month out of her paycheck. Also, as she now recognizes the value of building up her savings, she decides to use the $1,000 per month to make a payment of $300 (approximately the minimum payment) on her credit card and put the rest in a money market account.

Method 1:

She writes a check for $300 each month to the credit card company and puts $700 in her money market account. At the end of one year, her balance of funds available for emergencies looks like this:

Credit limit on credit card	$10,000
Subtract balance after paying $300 per month for 12 months	8,044
Funds available from credit card	1,956
Balance in money market account, including interest of $195	8,595
Total funds available	$10,551

Method 2:

She would have done better if she had used the whole $1,000 each month to reduce her credit card balance, as follows:

Credit limit on credit card	$10,000
Balance after paying $1,000 per month for 11 months (includes interest on $10,000)	0
Funds available from credit card	10,000
Balance in money market account (part of the 11th month and the 12th month payment of $1,000 plus interest	1,084
Total funds available	$11,084

Summary:

Funds available by method 2	$11,084
Subtract funds available by method 1	10,551
Additional funds available by using second method	$ 533

Figure 5.3 Winning Income from the Bank

Emergency Funds versus Short-term Investments

Up to this point, our focus has been primarily on emergency money, which is money you might need at a moment's notice. Emergency funds are often confused with what the financial people call *short-term investments,* and the basic definition of that term comes in two parts:

DEFINITION

- Short-term *is a nebulous concept. At this point, let's assume it means from tomorrow to one year from now.*
- *An investment is something into which you put your money with the expectation that it will increase in value by the time you want to withdraw it out of the investment.*

Investment Comes in Two Distinct Flavors

In both cases, you might receive the interest or earnings periodically over the months or years your money is invested.

1. Those that guarantee you will get all your money back, with the interest that your money earned, at some *future date.*
2. Those that guarantee you almost nothing but give you the *possibility* of greater earnings than you would get from a guaranteed investment.

Are short-term guaranteed investments suitable for emergency money? No. Why? Because a guaranteed investment promises only that you will receive all your money at some future date when the investment will *mature* on the *maturity* date. If you need cash before that date, you may not get all your invested money back.

Example: In September, Jerome struck oil in his backyard and was immediately paid many thousands of dollars by the neighborhood oil drilling company. Complex IRS rules are such that he does not need to pay $10,000 income tax on that money until the following April 15. He determines he should set aside $10,000 out of his earnings with which to pay that tax in April. He has several choices about where to keep it:

- In his mattress. This is not a good choice, mainly because of risk of fire. Also, mattresses pay no interest.
- In a bank money market fund, which might pay him 3 percent interest.
- In a six-month bank CD that pays 4 percent. (Jerome would earn $200 of interest.)
- In a U.S. Treasury bill that pays 5.5 percent, or $275 of interest. (A *Treasury bill* is not the kind of bill your dentist or the IRS sends you that says "please remit." It is an IOU from the U.S. Treasury to pay you on some future date but not until that date.)

Because it will put more money in his pocket, he buys the U.S. Treasury bill that will mature on April 10 and pay him $10,275.

Unfortunately, on January 10, Archie, Jerome's accountant, calls and admits to Jerome that he misinterpreted the IRS rules. Jerome has to pay the $10,000 on January 15. What can Jerome do? If he asks the U.S. Treasury to redeem his investment early, the folks at the Treasury may be sympathetic, but they can't redeem it early. Jerome will have to sell his Treasury bill to someone else. Fortunately, there is a market for these, but when Jerome, through his investment broker, attempts to sell his Treasury bill, he finds that the market is soft and he can receive only $9,975 for his $10,000 Treasury bill and the interest it has earned so far.

Obviously, Jerome would have been better off just to have put his money in a bank money market account. However, if Archie had not made a mistake, the Treasury bill would have earned more than the bank would have.

The point of this example is that, unless you are 99.9 percent sure that you will not need the money until a certain date, don't put your money where the whims of the marketplace may turn your investment into a loss if you need your money in a hurry.

In Chapter 6 we'll cover a relatively safe but long-term investment: real estate. In Chapter 7 there is more explanation about Treasury bills and other government securities. From there we go to more speculative investments in Chapter 8.

A bank CD has somewhat the same downside. However, you always know the amount of the penalty for an early withdrawal from a CD. The "penalty" for selling an investment in the marketplace is an unknown amount.

Real Estate—Where You Can Stash Your Long-term Money

INCLUDES

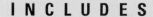

- Help in determining your risk tolerance

- Why your home perhaps is, or perhaps isn't, your best investment

- The costs of buying real estate

- Considerations about real estate brokers and agents

- When you should mortgage your property, even if you don't need to

- How to evaluate a variable-rate mortgage

- How to be wise about balloon mortgages

- Determine how much risk you can stand and how much you should stand. Also establish how far away your long-term investment horizon is. Together, these two factors determine the nature of your investments. *(p. 91)*

- Your house can be the best real estate investment if you plan to live in it for several years and if you pick the neighborhood carefully. (The 1997 tax law made most home ownership even more attractive.) *(p. 94)*

- When buying and selling real estate, remember that the real estate agent is an agent of the seller. If you are buying, take precautions, such as contracting with a buyer's agent. *(p. 96)*

- Owning rental real estate can build wealth and immediately reduce your income taxes somewhat. As in any business, a careful analysis of the property can keep you clear of most pitfalls. *(p. 100)*

We were brought up to believe that we should put something away for a rainy day. But now, given the dire predictions that Social Security and other economic support programs will go bankrupt, we are told that we have to save up for much more than an umbrella and a bowl of soup. We are supposed to pile up enough money to support us when we are too old to work. And that advice comes at a time in life when it takes every penny (and pennies from the bank) to feed, clothe, and educate the offspring.

The solution, as we again are often told, is to squeeze more out of our paycheck(s). But that won't be enough money to do the job. We also have to make it grow into a pot that will last until we are, perhaps, 100 years old.

Chapters 1 and 2 provide ideas on squeezing the paycheck. This and the following chapters cover how to fertilize and water the green paper stuff so it grows into a large dollar harvest over time. In other words, here we cover long-term investing, as distinguished from short-term emergency funds covered in Chapter 5.

How Long Is It to Harvest Time?
What Is Long Term?

If you are 20 years old, retirement is probably 45 or 50 years away, so that may be your long term. If you're 30, with a couple of young children, long term may be to the year the oldest enters college. If you're 80 years old, long term is probably 10 years. Whatever it is, it is not short term. That is, those investments into which you put your money for long-term growth should not be the same as those into which you put your short-term and emergency money.

What Is Your Risk Tolerance?

What is risk tolerance? Basically, it describes how much risk you are willing to take to make your money grow. If you have a very low risk tolerance, you prefer to keep your money where the government guarantees you will never lose any of it and where it will receive some interest income. If you have an extremely high tolerance for risk, you might take $100 to the roulette table at your neighborhood gambling casino and hope for some big winnings, although the odds are that you will lose.

Here are some questions that can help you decide what your risk tolerance is and what it perhaps should be:

- What is your age? If you're young, you have time and earning power in which to recover from losses, so you can have a fairly high tolerance for risk. If you are elderly, you may have neither the necessary earning power nor the time to recover from any losses, so you should take no risks.

- What is your earning power? If you earn barely enough to support yourself and your family, keep whatever you can save in a safe investment. If you have the skills or credentials to earn a high income, you can take more of a gamble (but preferably not roulette).

- What are your lifestyle preferences and requirements? Of course, most of us would prefer a lifestyle that is a little more comfortable and enjoyable than that which we have now, but what do we require? If you and your spouse can be happy in a shack in the woods, you can take more risk than if you must have the $500,000 home on the golf course.

- What are your responsibilities? If your children are grown and gone and if there is no prospect that you may have to contribute to the support of aging parents or other relatives, you can have a greater risk tolerance than if you have, or will have, the responsibility of supporting others.

- How close are you to the safety net? This one is a little harder to visualize, so let's look at John's situation. He and his wife were both 65 years old and, between Social Security and pensions, had about $20,000 in income. Their savings amounted to $10,000. In a safe investment, that $10,000 might earn $400 per year, which would be some extra money but not a significant amount. Also, when they reached the nursing home stage, that

$10,000 would be gone quickly in the charges for their care, and they would then be supported by the safety net of Supplemental Security Income (SSI). (That federal program would make up the difference between their income and the nursing home cost.) Therefore, John decided to take $5,000 of that savings and invest it in a higher-risk investment that might generate some funds they could enjoy in their retirement. Because they were so close to the safety net anyway, there was little harm in taking on more risk.

Probably someone could (or they may have already) put together a system of scoring your answers and come up with some kind of number that tells you what your risk level is. In my opinion, you will have a better handle on your risk tolerance if you mull over these factors and any others that come to mind, and then make a decision.

CAUTION

When thinking of risk, consider the risk of doing nothing or too little. If we have a moderate inflation rate of 3 percent per year, the first 3 percent that your money earns each year only keeps you even. If inflation goes above 3 percent, you will be losing ground. Remember that the loss-of-value risk is there.

Real Estate: A Good Place to Build Your Nest Egg

As someone said of real estate, "They aren't making any more of it, so it has to be a good investment." That's generally true. When you have a product that is out of production and buyers who are multiplying by the millions, the price is sure to go up—if it's in the right place. Obviously, that's not true of a plot in the middle of the desert or in a decaying part of a city. But if it's a place where you would like to live, it's probably in a good area.

The Best Real Estate Investment—Your Residence (Usually)

This is the one opportunity we all have to own residential property without having to worry about tenants and whether they will take care of the building and pay the rent. There are other advantages, and some disadvantages.

The Benefits of Owning Your House

- Once you lock in your mortgage, you know approximately how much cash it will take every month to live there. As time goes by and inflation makes living costs creep up, your house costs stay about the same. (I say "approximately" and "about" because some costs, such as taxes, utilities, and insurance, probably will increase.)
- You can maintain the good condition of your home so it should increase in value.
- It can become part of your retirement income through a reverse mortgage.

DEFINITION

A **reverse mortgage** is the opposite of a mortgage you incur to purchase a home. It is designed for older, retired people with small incomes and a paid-for house. If you fit this picture, a lender would take a mortgage from you, secured by your home, and then pay you a specific amount every month for a number of years. Or, you may be able to arrange to receive payments until you die. In either event, the lender becomes the owner of your house after the last payment. Fees can be exorbitant and mortgage terms misleading, so investigate carefully before using this source of cash. For consumer help, call the nonprofit National Center for Home Equity Conversion at 800-247-6553 or write the organization at 7373 147th Street, Room 115, Apple Valley, MN 55124.

- When you sell your residence, any capital gain, up to $500,000 on a joint return, may be tax-free.
- The IRS lets you deduct the interest portion of your mortgage, but see the later section on this subject.

The Advantages of Renting Your House (The Disadvantages of Owning It)

- You avoid risk that the house will lose its value. That can happen in areas where real estate values have risen quickly in the last few years and the bubble is about to break. It is also a risk if the neighborhood seems to be deteriorating.

- You avoid forking over money to contractors and repair people if the plumbing, electric, or heating/air conditioning become inoperative or the roof springs a leak.

- You don't have to pay for insurance on the building. You need worry only about insurance on your stuff that is in the house.

- Like a homeowner, you can lock in your housing expense for a number of years. Try to negotiate a one-year lease that is renewable at the same rental each year for several years. Most landlords and rental agencies will push a "standard" lease under your nose and tell you that the form is the "required" lease in the area. That is not true. If you are a desirable tenant (you pay your bills and look after your premises), you are in a position to negotiate any changes to the lease you want.

- You avoid the hassle and expense if you have to sell your house within two or three years of buying it. This can happen as a result of job change, growing family, or change in marital status. The costs of both buying and selling may offset any gain in value and the benefit of deductible interest. Among these costs are the following.

The Costs of Buying and Selling Your House

This subject is important enough to deserve some additional comments. The list of these costs includes:

- Commissions paid to real estate brokers
- Surveys
- Recording fees
- Title search and/or title insurance
- Mortgage processing fees
- Points: This is lump-sum interest that has to be paid at closing and is nonrefundable even if you soon pay off the mortgage by selling the house

- Repairs the buyer (or the city) requires when you sell the house
- Fees to the professional who prepares the documents and conducts the closing of the sale

These fees vary from state to state and between metropolitan areas within states, so there is no rule of thumb. If you buy through a real estate broker, he or she should give you an estimate of these fees when you make an offer on a house. However, that is too late. You need an estimate of these fees before you start looking at houses, especially if you think you might own the house for only a few years. Insist that the broker give you an estimate of these fees early in your house hunting. If you don't buy through a real estate broker, obtain what free information you can from a mortgage company. Then buy an hour of time from a real estate attorney to fill in the gaps in your knowledge.

Using a Real Estate Broker or Agent

There is little difference between a broker and an agent, except that having a broker's license requires more knowledge and experience. (An agent has to work under a broker's supervision.) For this discussion, we'll refer to both as "agent."

Remember that real estate agents are agents of the sellers. That means they are supposed to look after the seller's interest. (Sell the house for the best price.) That means they should paint the rosiest picture of the property they can, short of mis-representation. You can try to have a real estate agent in your corner by contracting with one to be a "buyer's agent." This person would have your interests as his or her primary concern. (You should be able to locate an agent who will perform this function by calling the local board of realtors.) The usual way a buyer's agent is compensated is by splitting the commission with the seller's agent. The problem with that, of course, is that there is just as much of an economic incentive for your agent to see you buy the property as there is for the seller's agent. Therefore, although it will be money out of your pocket, it may be worthwhile to hire a real estate agent for an hourly or flat fee for advice. In evaluating a neighborhood and its schools, a real estate agent should be more knowledgeable than other sources of advice, such as real estate attorneys and mortgage companies.

An agent who steers you away from a neighborhood that is near a park that holds open-air rock concerts is worth the fee.

Where and How to Borrow the Money You Need to Buy a House

Unless you are independently wealthy or you are older and have sold a "paid-for" house or have sold other assets, you are going to need to borrow some money.

CAUTION

If you have other assets, you may be tempted to borrow, using those as collateral and keeping your home free and clear. For tax reasons, that's not a good idea. If you use proceeds of a loan to buy your home, and the loan is not secured by a mortgage on your home, the interest is not deductible on your tax return.

Should You Take on a Mortgage Even If You Don't Have to?

This is a decision that depends on your risk level. If you can put your money to work and earn as much as the interest rate on your mortgage, it may be a good idea. This is particularly true if mortgage rates are low, as they are while I'm writing this. When interest rates rise later, you may be able to invest your funds at an interest rate that is higher than what you are paying on your mortgage. For instance, if you can sign a mortgage today with a 7.5 percent interest rate, and then next year buy a well-rated corporate bond paying 9 percent, you can make a profit of 1.5 percent on the mortgage company's money.

CAUTION

Do not use the proceeds of your home mortgage to buy tax-exempt state and municipal bonds. If you use your mortgage proceeds in that way, the tax law says you cannot deduct the interest on your mortgage.

Variable-Rate or Fixed-Rate Mortgage?

Here is another decision that rests in part on your risk or gambling tolerance level. If you expect to live in this particular house for the next 30 years and want a lid on most of your house payment for that time, go for the fixed rate mortgage.

If you expect to live in this house for only a few years, choosing a variable rate should get you into the house at a lower house payment amount, because variable mortgages come with a lower interest rate. The downside of this arrangement for you (and the upside for the mortgage company) is that, if the general level of interest rates rises, the interest rate on your mortgage can rise, so your house payment can rise. If you sell your house four or five years after buying it, this disadvantage of a variable rate may be of no consequence, for you will be out of the deal before the mortgage company can raise the rate significantly. To be certain that is the case, be sure your mortgage has these features:

- The interest rate remains the same for the first two or three years.
- The interest rate cannot increase by more than 1 or 2 percent each year after the initial locked-in rate.
- There is a cap, or maximum rate, that you can be required to pay at any time during the life of the mortgage. (Before you sign, be sure to find out what your payment will be at the maximum interest rate. Could you handle it?)
- There is no penalty, or only a very small penalty, for paying the mortgage off early. (That's so you can refinance the mortgage if rates go lower.)

Should You Sign a Balloon Mortgage?

Balloon mortgage loans, which can trip you up, work as in this example:

- You borrow $100,000.
- You agree to a 6 percent interest rate. (That rate is below the usual mort-gage rate at the time. That's the incentive for you to sign this mortgage.)
- You agree to monthly payments as if this were a 30-year mortgage, which is $599.55 for $100,000 at 6 percent. (Note that we are discussing the

payment that goes to pay down the mortgage *principal* and the interest. It does not include taxes, insurance, and so on.)

- However, the mortgage terms state that after five years (60 payments) you have to pay the remaining balance of the mortgage in one lump sum. That will be $93,054.36.

- When the five years are up, you find you have $37.86 in your bank account and $42.00 in your wallet. Even if you borrow from your retirement fund (a no-no), there is only $23,000 in it.

- If you're lucky, you can sell the house, find someone to lend you money via a new, replacement mortgage, or renegotiate the mortgage with your present mortgage company. What if the real estate market in your area is depressed and your home is now worth only $85,000? Who is going to lend you $93,000 on a property worth $85,000?

   If you lack a rich aunt, you're in a pickle.

Don't sign up for an arrangement like this that can put you in a no-escape box. It is probable that, because your present mortgage company does not want to foreclose on a property with a value that is less than the mortgage balance, they will negotiate a continuation of the mortgage loan with you. However, do you think there is any chance they will continue payments at the 6 percent interest rate? Of course not. The mortgage company has you in a corner, so it can charge whatever it likes. You could find your payment is doubled! In effect, this arrangement amounts to a variable rate mortgage with no limit on what the mortgage company can charge after the first five years.

There is another way around this dilemma. If, before you sign the mortgage, you make sure it has a "reset" clause, you can be a little more comfortable. This clause guarantees you that you can refinance the mortgage, at a rate only slightly above the going market rate at the five-year point, even if the value of your home is less than the balance of the mortgage. Even without the reset clause, the mortgage company might refinance your debt anyway, but there would be no limit on the interest it could charge.

What does this refinancing mean in hard numbers? If that $93,054 were refinanced at 10 percent for the remaining 300 months, the payment would increase to $845.59.

Think long and hard before you sign up for buying your dream house on a balloon, only to see it punctured!

Investing In and Owning Rental Property

In times of rampaging inflation, such as in the late 1970s and early 1980s, real estate can be an excellent investment, for real estate values tend to increase as fast as the level of prices increases. At other times, it's a good investment. Houses, duplexes, and apartment buildings in desirable neighborhoods never become worthless, so if you own rental real estate, you always own something of value. Beyond that, there is some tax incentive to own rental property.

Make Money from Rental Property and Cut Your Taxes

Unfortunately, to explain how this happens, we have to delve into a rather dry area than only an accountant could love. It's called *depreciation*.

The Depreciation Factor

Example: Jerry bought a rental house for $120,000 and determined that the house was worth $100,000 and the land was worth $20,000. The theory held by accountants and the IRS is that the land will always be there, but the house will wear out and fall down someday. No one knows when that will actually happen, but the IRS settles any arguments with a rule that says you can consider that residential rental buildings will last 27.5 years. In order to keep Jerry from deducting the whole $100,000 cost of the house in the year in which he bought it, the IRS says he has to allocate that cost to each of the years the house is expected to last. And that process is what is called *depreciation*. (I have no idea how they came up with that 27.5 number.) So, Jerry divides the $100,000 cost of the house by 27.5 and comes up with a yearly depreciation expense of $3,636.

Notice that Jerry never writes a check for $3,636 to the IRS. It is not part of his cash flow. What he does write checks for and what he collects in rent are listed in Figure 6.1 under the heading of "Cash Flow." The numbers from the operation of the rental property indicate he would have a cash drain (outflow) of $1,000 during the first year. However, there is more for him to compute.

The numbers under the next heading of "Computation of Tax Effect" in Figure 6.1 appear to be similar to the cash flow numbers, but these are the numbers that

Situation		
Cost of building		$100,000
Cost of land		20,000
Total cost of property		120,000
Subtract down payment (20%)		24,000
Finance by 30-year mortgage at 8% interest		$ 96,000
Cash picture (cash flow), first year		
Rental received at $825 per month		$ 9,900
Subtract cash flow out:		
Mortgage payment	$8,400	
Real estate tax	1,000	
Insurance	500	
Maintenance and repairs	1,000	
Total outflow of cash		10,900
Negative cash flow before tax effect		(1,000)
Add: tax benefit of this rental property (explained below)		1,070
Positive cash flow		$ 70
Computation of tax effect (numbers that go on federal individual income tax return)		
Rental received at $825 per month		$ 9,900
Subtract expenses:		
Depreciation	3,636	
Interest on mortgage	7,587	
Real estate tax	1,000	
Insurance	500	
Maintenance and repairs	1,000	
Total expenses		13,723
Loss on tax return		(3,823)
Multiply by tax bracket (See the Appendix for yours)		x 28%
Reduction in income tax due to rental property		
(Carried to cash flow computation above.)		($ 1,070)

Figure 6.1 Computation of After-tax Income from Rental Property
      Investment

go on Jerry's tax return, and they are not the same as the cash flow. Specifically, they are the following:

- The part of the mortgage payment that reduces the total debt (the principal) of the mortgage is not deductible. Only the interest portion ($7,587 in the first year) is deductible.

- As pointed out earlier, depreciation is not a cash item, but it is deductible on the tax return, so it appears in this tax section.

The result is a tax loss on paper of $3,823. Because Jerry is in the 28 percent tax bracket, that loss results in a reduction of his income tax of $1,070. Because a reduction of tax is like extra money in his pocket, that wipes out the cash outflow, as indicated in the last two lines of the cash flow computation.

If Jerry made these same computations for the 15th year, cranking in a computation for inflation of 2 percent per year, he would have a positive inflow of cash of $1,550. Unfortunately, his tax picture would have reversed, due mainly to less interest expense. So, after paying $104 tax, his final cash flow is an inflow of $1,445.

In year 30, his final cash flow is $2,436. In year 31 and later, it gets much better. There are no more mortgage payments; only expenses for taxes, insurance, and maintenance remain.

So, for an investment of the $24,000 down payment, by the time Jerry retires he will have a rental property free and clear, worth perhaps $200,000 (reflecting inflation) and rental income of close to $20,000 per year, with few expenses. Not bad, but read on before you run out to buy real estate.

Some Other Considerations About Rental Property Ownership

- Renting to the *right* tenants is critical. Irresponsible tenants who fail to pay the rent and wreck the property can render the property a bad investment. Before advertising "for rent," put the property in prime condition with cleaner and paint, and check references on tenants who apply.

- Do you expect to stay in the same area most of your life, or are you subject to job transfers or other reasons to move around the country, or around the world? If you do move out of the area in which you own rental property, you will have to hire a rental management company to keep your property occupied with good tenants and to contract for necessary repairs. That management costs money, so owning rental property is less attractive for those of us who move frequently.

- There is a limit on how much of your losses from rental property you can deduct from your regular income on your income tax return. Basically, that limit is $25,000, and you can have the full benefit of that tax shelter only if your total income is less than $100,000. (There are more rules involved; they are in my previous book, *Taxes for Busy People*. A conference with your tax preparer/advisor *before* you buy rental property would be a good idea.)

Suggested Action Before You Buy Rental Property

- Check rental rates *yourself.* Find properties that are similar to the one you are considering, and call the owners or agents for quotes on the rental.
- Have an independent accountant project the cash flow and tax consequences of ownership for each property you consider buying. (Not all property works out to be a good investment, as did our example.) The real estate agent who is selling the property may have already prepared such a projection, but the agent's interest is in selling the property. You should still have an accountant review the projection. If you use an accountant to prepare your tax forms, that person would be a logical choice.

Real Estate Investment Trusts (REITs)

Buying a share of one of these financial creatures is a method of investing in real estate even if you move around. As an owner, you are far removed from the nitty-gritty concerns of managing real property. These REITs, at least the ones you would want to invest in, are so similar to stock mutual funds that they are covered in Chapter 9.

Make Your Money Grow: Relatively Safe Investments

INCLUDES

- How your money can earn more money

- The risks involved in investments

- The returns on U.S. savings bonds are new and improved

- What to do when your savings bonds mature

- How to invest in the U.S. government and save on income taxes

- Other ways to invest in and earn interest from the U.S. government

- How to get cash from your government bonds when you need it

- Bonds that are tax free

- When you should invest in tax-free bonds

- When you should buy bonds issued by corporations

- The lure of "junk bonds"

105

- The money you have saved can earn more money. How much depends on where you invest it and how much risk you will, and should and should not, take. *(p. 108)*

- The U.S. government's Series EE bonds keep getting better. Now they pay interest at rates close to comparable investments. They come in small pieces, are easy to buy, and have some tax-saving features when you exchange them for Series HH bonds or cash them in and use the proceeds for education. *(p. 109)*

- Treasury bills, notes, and bonds are suitable for some investors who need to invest a significant amount of cash for varying periods. *(p. 113)*

- The new federal government inflation-indexed bonds are appealing to those who fear a return someday to very high inflation rates. *(p. 113)*

- State and municipal bonds generate interest income that is not taxed. Therefore, they are worthy of consideration by those who are in a high enough tax bracket. *(p. 116)*

- Corporate bonds can generate higher interest rates and the opportunity to generate gain in the value of the bonds if conditions change. But they can also generate losses. *(p. 119)*

Where to put money so it will be safe has always been a challenge for us, ever since the cave people started using doughnut-shaped rocks or lions' teeth as a medium of exchange. Now, if you believe the U.S. government will make good on its promises and be around for many years, the physical storage is not a problem. You can keep your money in a bank, where the government guarantees your money up to $100,000 as long as the bank is insured by the FDIC. Or you can simply invest your money by loaning it to the federal government.

Yes, those alternatives make sure that no one will tear open your mattress and find your stash of cash. But the banks and the government don't necessarily protect you against a slower thief that is just as dangerous as the guy working over your mattress with a knife: inflation. To keep money safe from that, you need to put it where it will earn more, and the more it earns, the better your protection from inflation. At this writing, in the late 1990s, inflation is viewed as almost nonexistent. Yet, over many years, inflation has seemed to persist at around 3 percent, and even at that low rate, prices will double in 25 years.

Money Your Money Earns

For this explanation, think of your money in terms of what it could buy or be converted into. If $10,000 of your money were turned into an automobile, which would be easy to do, and Louie, your brother-in-law, wanted to use it for a month, you would (at least, you should) expect him to pay rent for the month. There is no difference when that hypothetical vehicle is still money in your pocket. If you loan it out, you should receive rent. In the financial world, that rent is called interest, and it can be viewed as being composed of three factors:

1. The rental value of the money. Over many years, it seems to average around 3 percent, if it is certain you will be paid back.
2. An additional amount to cover the loss of purchasing power caused by inflation. Because you cannot purchase goods and services with the money you have loaned out, the borrower should reimburse you for the purchasing power lost during the length (term) of the loan.
3. An amount to compensate you for the risk that you are taking, including the risk that the borrower might not pay you back.

As there is little you can do to change factors one and two, how much you can make your money earn depends on how much risk you are willing to take and how much you should take.

How Much Risk Should You Take?

This is one of those questions that can best be answered by another question: How much do you depend on the money you're investing and on the results (interest) of the earnings? If the money is what you have set aside for next month's rent or to pay your health insurance, you cannot afford to take any risk beyond what is inherent in just living.

If losing the money would not be a disaster, you can take risks, and that could make you wealthy. Obviously, risk is not an all-or-nothing situation. It comes in many, many levels and flavors, all the way from loaning money to the federal government, where the only risk is loss of purchasing power, to investing in fake gold mines. A good way to avoid exposure to both risks—inflation and speculative ventures—is to invest some of your money in each of several levels of risk.

Safe Investments: Government Bonds and Similar Places to Put Your Money

It hasn't been many years since most of us pooh-poohed U.S. savings bonds because the interest was too low to keep up with inflation. In other words, if your money was growing by an interest rate of 3 percent per year and inflation was growing at 6 percent per year, your money was shrinking by 3 percent per year in terms of purchasing power. It is not how many dollars you have but how much purchasing power you have that counts.

Savings Bonds Today (Series EE)

Savings bonds have been improved several times over the years, for the federal government tries to make it more attractive for us to loan money to it. (The government does have to finance the deficits.)

New Interest Rates

Since May 1, 1997, the interest on newly issued savings bonds has been based on the market yield of five-year Treasury securities (which are discussed later), so the old policy of keeping interest rates low for the first five years no longer applies. The rate is adjusted every six months on May 1 and November 1, and that rate applies to all bonds issued after May 1, 1997, until November 1. In other words, if you bought savings bonds in November 1997, they will earn interest at the rate set on November 1 of 5.59 percent. On May 1, 1998, the same bonds will earn at a different rate, depending on what the financial markets will pay for Treasury securities then.

Because the rate of interest is 90 percent of a rate that is set in the financial markets, and because the auction nature of the financial market almost always sets a rate that is more than the inflation rate, it is now almost impossible for you to lose purchasing power by investing in Series EE U.S. savings bonds.

Penalty If You Cash in a Bond Within Five Years of Purchase

Although these bonds now earn market rates right from the start, there is some penalty if you cash them in during the first five years of their life: You will lose three months' worth of interest. So, if there is a good chance you will need cash from your bond within the next two years, you may be better off in a bank money market account. If you won't need it for more than two years, you may be better off putting your money in EE bonds and paying the penalty than you would be if you put the money in a bank. Even if you keep the bond for only two years, you would still come out ahead over a savings account.

Double Your Money Is Guaranteed

You still purchase bonds for half of their face amount. (A $50 bond costs $25 today.) Although it is very unlikely, if interest rates are so low that your bond does not reach its face value in 17 years, the government will make up the difference.

Example: You pay $25 for a $50 bond today. Over the years, the interest accumulates, making your bond worth more every year. However, interest rates are so low that the bond is worth only $45 in 17 years. It doesn't matter; the government will still pay you $50 for the bond at that time. If, on the other hand, the bond is worth $75, you can cash it in for the $75. (You do not have to cash in the bond in 17 years. It will continue to earn interest until 30 years have passed since you purchased it.)

Tax Advantages of Series EE Bonds

- You do not need to pay tax on the interest, because it is added to the value of your bond each year. Instead, when you cash in the bond, you pay the tax on the interest earned since day one.

- If you don't want to pay tax on that interest when the bond matures and you don't need the cash, you can exchange the Series EE bonds for Series HH. That doesn't make the tax go away, but it defers it until you cash in the HH bonds. However, you will have to pay income tax on the interest that the HH bonds pay you twice a year.

- You can, if you meet the qualifications, make the income tax on the EE bonds go away permanently if you cash the bonds in and use the proceeds for higher education for yourself, your spouse, or your dependents. You must have bought the bonds in your name (not in a child's name), and you must have been at least 24 years old when you purchased them. Also, the amount of tax that is forgiven diminishes if your income is over $50,850 if you are single, or over $65,850 if you are married. Also, if you are married, you must file a joint return.

How to Purchase Series EE Bonds

The bonds are issued by a Federal Reserve bank, but you can make your purchase through almost any bank or credit union. Some banks and credit unions offer an automatic purchase arrangement. Also, some employers will purchase savings bonds for employees through a payroll deduction program. (If you never see the money, you won't miss it quite so much.) The bonds come in several denominations from $50 to $10,000.

Series HH Savings Bonds

Unlike the Series EE bonds, Series HH bonds pay interest to you every six months, and that interest is taxable in the year in which you receive it. The interest rate, currently 4 percent, is set when an HH bond is issued and does not change for at least 10 years.

The one advantage of HH bonds is that they offer a way to defer the income tax on EE bonds when they mature, as explained under the EE bond section.

*A handy option for your
retirement date.*

Although you cannot directly purchase HH bonds, you can buy EE bonds and exchange them for HH bonds any time after you have owned the EE bonds for six months.

The Quandary: Should You Exchange EE Bonds for HH Bonds?

If you make this exchange, you will defer some income tax, but you will be in an investment that pays only 4 percent. Is putting off the tax man worth the lower interest rate?

Example: When Sally retired, she had EE bonds with a value of $10,000, for which she had paid $5,000 some years ago. In other words, she had taxable interest income of $5,000 if she cashed in the bonds. She also had some other retirement income, so she was in the 28 percent income tax bracket. She wondered if she should exchange her EE bonds for HH bonds. She could have hired a financial wizard to figure this out, but she decided to compute it herself with paper and calculator. Her computations are shown in Figure 7.1.

It appears that, if Sally planned to keep the funds invested for at least 18 years at 6 percent or better, she would be ahead to cash in her EE bonds now and go for other investments with a higher rate of interest. Actually, that point is reached somewhat sooner, as there is still a tax liability on the $5,000 of interest earned on the EE bonds if she exchanges them for HH bonds. That tax will have to be paid someday.

Other Ways You Can Loan Money to the U.S. Government

Series EE bonds are the vehicle most people use for investing in the federal government. For those people who do better with automatic deductions from their paycheck or bank account, Series EE bonds are the only way to go. Even people on a tight budget will usually not miss the deduction of $25 that will buy a savings bond.

However, if you already have saved up several thousand dollars in your nest egg, and you want to be sure you can't lose any of your money, there are other U.S. government securities that may offer you a higher interest rate. These are IOUs from the government that state that after so many days, months, or years, you will be paid back all your money. In some cases, you will be paid the interest along with the return of the principal. In other cases, you'll be paid the interest periodically while you hold the IOU.

*The buzzword for IOUs is
"Treasury securities."*

	Do Not Exchange Bonds	Exchange Bonds
After-tax proceeds if she cashes in EE Bonds rather than exchange them for HH Bonds:		
Cash she will receive	$10,000	$10,000
Income tax (28% times $5,000 in interest income)	1,400	0
Cash left after paying income tax	$ 8,600	$10,000
At interest rate of	6%	4%
Cash left after paying income tax	$ 8,600	$10,000
Interest, year 1	372	288
Interest, year 2	372	288
Interest, year 3	372	288
Interest, year 4	372	288
Interest, year 5	372	288
Interest, year 6	372	288
Interest, year 7	372	288
Interest, year 8	372	288
Interest, year 9	372	288
Interest, year 10	372	288
Interest, year 11	372	288
Interest, year 12	372	288
Interest, year 13	372	288
Interest, year 14	372	288
Interest, year 15	372	288
Interest, year 16	372	288
Interest, year 17	372	288
Interest, year 18	372	288
Total received for bond and interest	$15,287	$15,184

Figure 7.1 Should an Individual Cash in Her EE Bonds or Exchange Them for HH Bonds?

Treasury Bills

Treasury bills are not like those your dentist sends you. You buy these bills from the U.S. Treasury, and they are actually U.S. government IOUs issued for a term of one year or less. You don't receive an interest check if you invest in these, but you buy the bill for less than its face amount (the discount). When it matures and you cash it in, you receive the face amount of the bill. The discount when you bought it is the interest, and it is taxable when the bill matures. Therefore, you can defer income taxes on the interest for up to almost a year. The minimum purchase amount for Treasury bills is $10,000, and in increments of $1,000 above that. There are varying lengths of time to maturity but never for more than a year.

Treasury Notes

These government IOUs come with a specific interest rate, and the interest is paid twice a year. They are issued in maturities of up to 10 years. The minimum purchase is $5,000 if the maturity is less than five years and $1,000 if the maturity is from five to 10 years.

Treasury Bonds

As with notes, the interest on Treasury bonds is paid twice a year. The minimum purchase is $1,000, and the term to maturity is 10 years or more.

Treasury Inflation-indexed Securities

These are new securities, first issued in 1997. The face amount (the amount you will receive when the bonds mature) will be increased to reflect increases in the Consumer Price Index each year. Because that feature replaces the inflation factor that is included in most interest rates, the interest rates on these bonds is substantially less than on other government bonds. However, when interest is paid (twice a year), the rate is computed on the adjusted face amount.

Example: You buy a $10,000 inflation-adjusted bond paying 3 percent per year. In the first year, you will receive $300 interest. In the second year, when inflation has run wild at 10 percent, the face amount of the bond is adjusted by 10 percent to $11,000. Now your interest checks for the second year will be $330 (3 percent of $11,000).

There is a tax downside to these inflation-indexed bonds. The annual increase in the face value ($1,000 in the example) is taxable income to the owner of the bond, even though the owner does not receive that $1,000 in cash until the bond matures years in the future.

How Do You Buy and Sell Treasury Securities?

If you buy Treasury securities when they are issued and keep them until they mature, you have a choice. You can transact your bond business directly with the U.S. Treasury, or you can do the same through a securities broker. If you use a broker, be sure to find out what commissions you will pay.

There are markets for the securities. In other words, if you need cash, you can sell the security in the marketplace at any time before it matures. Of course, depending on the market, you may find you have a loss when you sell it this way, because the government guarantees you against loss only if you keep the security until it matures. The government does not participate in the buying and selling of existing securities in this *secondary* market. You can find current prices and the *yield* of government securities in financial newspapers such as *The Wall Street Journal.* If you do buy or sell in the secondary market, you do so through a securities broker. The U.S. Treasury does not participate in that marketplace.

What Is Yield and How Is It Calculated?

The answer is best explained by example.

Example: Jack bought a note (an IOU), issued by the country of Upperplate, on January 1. He paid $10,000 for the note, which had a stated value (face value) of $10,000 and an interest rate of 5 percent per year. It would mature on December 31, when it would pay the owner of the note $10,000 plus interest of $500.

An hour after he bought the note, Jack came upon a good deal on a used Porsche and immediately needed his $10,000 back.

His friend Phyllis was also going to buy a $10,000 note issued by the Upperplate Treasury, but she had procrastinated until late in the day. Then, when Jack told her that he needed to sell his note, she offered to pay him $9,500 for it. Thirsting for the Porsche, Jack accepted her deal. Mary bought the bond for $9,500 and registered the fact that she was the new owner with the Upperplate Treasury.

What interest rate did Phyllis earn on this note? The treasurer of Upperplate didn't care about what price she paid Jack for the note. The treasurer would write a check for $10,500 to whoever owned the bond on December 31. Therefore, Phyllis earned an interest rate computed as follows:

Interest received ÷ investment = $500 ÷ $9,500 = 0.0526

Converting that decimal number to a percentage = 5.26%

In other words, the *yield* depends on the price an owner pays for the IOU. It is not necessarily the face value of the bond.

The yield calculation in this example was fairly simple. It does get more complicated when the debt securities are held for just part of a year. It is further complicated when securities are issued at a *discount*, as are Treasury bills. That is, if you buy a new, one-year, 5 percent, $10,000 Treasury bill from the U.S. Treasury, you don't pay $10,000 but only $9,523.81. When the bill matures in one year, you receive $10,000 from the Treasury. The difference of $476.19 ($10,000 minus $9,523.81) is the interest, which is 5 percent of $9,523.81. A further complication is that this computation is theory. The price for new-issue Treasury bills is actually determined by public auction, as are prices in the secondary market.

EXPERT ADVICE

Do you need to be a PhD in math in order to compute yield? No. The financial newspapers list the available government securities, their current prices, and the yield you would receive if you bought them that day and held them until they matured.

IOU Prices, IOU Yields: Which Is Which?

As you can see from the Jack and Phyllis example, there is an interrelationship between the price and the yield of an IOU. Because Phyllis bought at a lower price, she received a higher yield. This is a relationship that applies to all IOUs, regardless of who issues them—the government, a business, or your Aunt Martha. If the price of the debt instrument (the IOU) goes up, the yield comes down, and vice versa.

That rule applies starting the minute you buy the IOU. Debt instruments you own will always yield the same percentage to you as they did when you bought them.

Where and How to Buy U.S. Treasury Securities

You can purchase Treasury Securities through commercial banks and through securities brokers. You can also buy them directly from the U.S. Treasury. The source of forms and detailed information is the Federal Reserve bank serving your area.

EXPERT ADVICE

If you have access to the Internet, you can find much additional information at the web site of the U.S. Treasury's Bureau of the Public Debt (http://www.publicdebt.treas.gov/). Or you can write to the Bureau of the Public Debt, P.O. Box 1328, Parkersburg, WV 26106-1328, and request the booklet, Buying Treasury Securities.

Bonds Issued by State and Local Governments

The attractive feature of these debt instruments is that the interest on them is not subject to federal income tax. Also, if you buy these IOUs that are issued by governments within the state you live in, they are usually not subject to state income tax. Because of that, they sell at a price that generates a lower yield than do IOUs that pay taxable interest.

Should You Buy Tax-exempt Bonds?

You can find the answer this way:

1. Find a quote (from the newspaper or your broker) of the yield for a taxable bond that meets your requirements for maturity date.
2. Determine your federal tax bracket from the table in the Appendix of this book. Add the tax rate for any state income tax you pay.
3. Compute the percentage—that is, 100 percent minus your tax rate.
4. Multiply the taxable yield of the bond by the percentage you found in Step 3. That is the yield to compare with that of a tax-exempt bond.

The formulas for this computation follow.

To find the equivalent nontaxable yield of a taxable yield:

(100% − total tax rate) × taxable yield = equivalent nontaxable yield

To find the equivalent taxable yield of a nontaxable yield:

Nontaxable yield ÷ (100% − total tax rate) = equivalent taxable yield

Figure 7.2 is an example of the calculation.

Step 1:	Enter yield of taxable bond.	6.00%
Step 2:	Determine federal income tax rate from appendix.	31.00
Step 3:	Determine state income tax rate if considering bonds also exempt from state tax. Otherwise, this number is zero.	5.00
Step 4:	Total tax rate (add results of Steps 2 and 3).	36.00
Step 5:	Subtract total tax rate from 100%.	64.00
Step 6:	Multiply taxable yield (Step 1) by result of Step 5; this is the yield of a tax-exempt bond that would generate the same after-tax income as the taxable yield in Step 1.	3.84%
	For the reverse computation, these are the steps:	
Step 1:	Enter yield of tax-exempt bond.	4.00%
Step 2:	Determine federal income tax rate from appendix.	31.00
Step 3:	Determine state income tax rate if considering bonds also exempt from state tax. Otherwise, this number is zero.	5.00
Step 4:	Total tax rate (add results of Steps 2 and 3).	36.00
Step 5:	Subtract total tax rate from 100%.	64.00
Step 6:	Divide the tax-exempt yield (Step 1) by result of Step 4; this is the yield of a taxable bond that would generate the same after-tax income as the tax-exempt yield in Step 1.	6.25%

Figure 7.2 Computation of Taxable versus Tax-exempt Yield from Bonds

CAUTION

Some inexperienced (or not very smart) investment brokers will encourage clients to buy securities with tax-exempt income when those clients are in a tax bracket that is too low. Such clients would be ahead if they received a higher interest rate and paid the income tax.

Make your own calculations. Obtain information about yield, maturity, rating of bond issuer (see the next section) from your broker, but do your own calculations of the tax impact.

Are Municipal Bonds Safe?

If you invest in bonds from most state, county, and municipal governments, you can feel reasonably secure in expecting your interest payments and repayment of your investment at maturity. However, there are exceptions. At one time there was doubt that New York City could meet its obligations, and more recently, Orange County, California, had severe financial problems.

How can you tell which state or city is financially strong? No, you don't need to wade through all the published financial details. There are services that rate the strength of these political entities. They are Standard & Poor's and Moody's Investor's Services. Both supply annual information and frequent updates.

Your broker can help you interpret what these services say and how they rate municipal bonds, or you can find at least one of these services in most libraries. If you have Internet access, you can get some information from the services at the following addresses, although you will still need to visit your library or call your broker to get specific rating information.

Standard & Poor's: http://www.ratings.com

Moody's Investor Services: http://www.moodys.com

Notes and Bonds Issued by Corporations (Not Quite the U.S. Treasury)

Like the government, many corporations sell their IOUs to investors for varying lengths of time. Also, like the value of Treasury bills, notes, and bonds (except the EE and HH savings bonds), the value of corporate bonds varies with the whim of the financial marketplace. Unlike government IOUs, bonds issued by corporations are not generated in one place but in the executive suites of hundreds of corporations. Their terms vary greatly, and covering them in any detail would fill a separate book. Nevertheless, a few basic facts can help you decide if any of your hard-saved dollars belong in these securities.

Why Buy Bonds Issued by Corporations?

Basically, corporate bonds are riskier than federal government bonds are, so they pay a higher interest rate.

Will the Corporate Bonds Be Good When They Mature?

That depends on the financial health of the corporation. If the business comes upon hard times and can't pay its suppliers and others, it probably cannot pay the people (called *bondholders*) who loaned it money by buying its bonds. Obviously, the further away the maturity date, the higher the risk, so bonds with a longer stretch of time to maturity usually pay a higher interest rate.

Can I Get My Money Out Before Maturity?

Yes, but not from the corporation. You can sell corporate bonds through your broker in the market. You will probably receive either more or less than you paid for the bonds, and that will affect the yield you receive.

What Are Convertible Bonds?

These are, in a way, a combination of a bond and a stock. They are covered later after we have discussed investments in stocks.

These bonds are a place for only your "gambling" money.

Are "Junk" Bonds a Good Deal?

"Junk" bonds are sold by companies that are not financially strong. They pay a high rate of interest because of the risk involved. Not only do you win from high interest rates, but if the company survives and becomes stronger, the market value of the bonds will increase and you could profit handsomely. On the other hand, if the company goes down the drain, you lose your investment.

This ends our discussion of debt instruments, which is the buzzword for IOUs. From here we move to Chapter 8 and into securities (common stock). If you own such securities, you are a part owner of a business.

8

Common Stocks—Can You Make Money in the Stock Market?

INCLUDES

- What are common stocks?

- How you can make money In the stock market

- Explanations of dividends and capital gains

- How stock market profits are taxed

- What determines a stock's price?

- What are the risks of buying stock?

- How to reduce the risks

- Where to find help on understanding investment in stocks

- Help in selecting a stockbroker

- What to avoid: stock market activities that are just gambling activities

FAST FORWARD

- As a stockholder, you are a part owner of a business. You may share handsomely in successes, but if there are failures, you will be the last to salvage any money out of the deal. *(p. 123)*

- Your tax bite will be less if you invest for capital gains rather than dividends. When possible, buy after the ex-dividend date. *(p. 127)*

- Many factors underlie the price of a stock, but ultimately it's the auction activities of the stock markets that determine the price. *(p. 133)*

- The stock market of the 1990s is far different from that of the 1920s. The safeguards now in place make the possibility of a repeat of the 1929 market crash extremely remote. *(p. 137)*

- There's an abundant supply of advice about the stock market, but the best source is your own self-education. Investment clubs and investor associations can help. *(p. 138)*

- Stockbrokers come with a full range of services and commission costs. Pick the type that provides the level of service you need. Paying higher commissions for services you don't use is a waste of money. Scrimping on services you should have to save commissions can also waste your money by the unnecessary losses you incur. *(p. 138)*

- Avoid the gambling areas: short-term trading and derivatives. *(p. 140)*

In this chapter, we move from money that you loan to some organization to money with which you actually buy part of a business. As is the case with any business owner, from the owner of the neighborhood hardware store to all the owners of General Motors, you assume more risk. You could become very wealthy owning all or part of a business, or you could become very broke.

But there are differences between the small business owner and those who own a share of a large corporation. The small business owner is usually active in the business. He or she makes a time commitment as well as a financial commitment. On the other hand, most of the people who own a little bit of General Motors have no idea about how to run an automobile assembly plant. They are otherwise employed, so they depend on the hired executives and managers to build the cars.

This chapter is for the latter group of owners—those who are not active in the business of which they own a few shares. The division of ownership among thousands of people is usually accomplished by setting up the business as a corporation, and what that means to an investor is where we start.

The Corporation—It Makes Sharing Ownership Easy

As would any good business school, we'll start with a case history.

Alice, Bart, and Connie decided to start a business manufacturing cardboard boats. Their logic was the surplus of used cardboard that fills every dumpster in town. They designed a factory to produce the boats and made a list of the cutting and gluing machines they would need. The total cost of the machines and supplies was $100,000. Unfortunately, each of the three entrepreneurs had only $10,000 available. They asked the bank for a loan, but the loan officer was unimpressed with the product idea. However, Alice's aunt Wilhelmina came to the rescue. She agreed to loan the enterprise $70,000.

Larry, the attorney they retained, set up the legal form of the business as a corporation called Soggy Boats, Incorporated. To each of the three owners (Alice, Bart, and Connie) he issued 1,000 shares of stock, and each share had a stated value of $10. Because a total of 3,000 shares was issued, the stock certificate for 1,000 shares that each of the owners (stockholders) now had was what documented their one-third share of the business.

To Wilhelmina he issued a $70,000 bond on which she was to receive interest of 12 percent per year, with her $70,000 investment to be repaid to her when the bond matured in 10 years.

The corporation went into production. The boats they produced had appealing lines. They sat on their trailers with decorum. But when they were launched into the water, they tended to soak it up, wrinkle, and submerge. Prospective boat owners saw this fiasco at the launching ramps, so sales fell off to nothing, and the business had to close.

There was only $500 left in the business checking account and the cash drawer, but Alice, Bart, and Connie managed to sell the used cutting and gluing machines for $25,000. Who properly received the $25,500 when the business closed?

The owners (stockholders) received zero.

Wilhelmina received the $25,500.

Why was the money disbursed this way? Because Wilhelmina was a bondholder, or creditor, of the corporation. When a corporation goes out of business, it is the bondholders (and any other creditors) who must be paid *in full* before the stockholders receive even a penny. That is one of the reasons that owning stock is riskier than owning bonds.

Let's change the facts of the story. Suppose Alice, Bart, and Connie found a way to waterproof and strengthen the cardboard. Their new process was an economical way to build boats, so they undersold all the competition. The business grew until it was worth $30 million in 10 years. That meant that the 1,000 shares of stock owned by the three shareholders was worth $10 million, and each share of stock was worth $10,000.

Wilhelmina's bond matured and the corporation paid her $70,000. She didn't share in the phenomenal growth of the corporation. Remember, she was a creditor, not an owner.

Although Alice, Bart, and Connie now were each worth $10 million, their worth was composed entirely of stock in Soggy Boats, Incorporated. They each wanted some cash so that they could enjoy the finer things of life. Therefore, they split each share of stock into 1,000 new shares of stock. Now there were 3 million shares issued, and each of the three owned 1 million shares. They went through the red tape involved, and each sold, through the stock market, 400,000 of his or her 1 million shares to many other people for $10 per share of stock.

Tony, who had used a Soggy boat and liked it, wrote a check for $1,000 to buy 100 of the new shares at $10 each when they were first put up for sale by the original owners. The next week, Delores thought the company would grow even larger and more profitable, so through her stockbroker, she bought Tony's 100 shares at $11 per share for $1,100. Tony made a gain of $100 on his $1,000 investment in one week, which is not bad. However, Delores kept the stock for another 10 years, and it became worth $900 per share. (Tony should have held on.)

This story illustrates several points about common stocks and investing in them. These points and other concepts are covered in the following sections.

Who Gets Paid First (Priorities)?

If a corporation has losses and other financial problems, so that it becomes insolvent with not enough money to pay all its bills, the creditors have to be paid *in full* before anything is paid to the stockholders. That means that the bondholders are to be repaid not only the face value of the bonds but also any interest that may be owed to them.

If, in the normal course of business, the corporation is short of cash and cannot pay the interest on the bonds, it is prohibited from paying any dividends (defined in the next section) to stockholders. Not only must the creditors, including bondholders, be paid back the money they invested when they bought their bonds; they must also be paid all the interest that may be owed to them before the stockholders are paid anything.

Who has to cough up the bucks to pay the bondholders if there is not enough left in the corporate treasury? Fear not; as a stockholder, you are not liable. One of the reasons for organizing a business as a corporation is that the owners of the business, as stockholders, do not have liability for the debts of the corporation. (That applies to General Motors and to Hanks Hardware, Incorporated, down the street.)

Money Invested in Stocks Should Earn Money (Dividends)

As owners of a corporation, stockholders take on the risk that the corporation will or will not be profitable. Therefore, they do not receive guaranteed periodic payments, as bondholders receive interest. Instead, stockholders receive dividends, which are paid by the decision (or whim) of the board of directors. Actually, most of the larger publicly held corporations try to be consistent, paying as much or more in dividends every year as they paid in the previous years. That keeps the stockholders happy so that they don't sell their stock, and that keeps the price of the stock up.

DEFINITION

All corporations have a board of directors that is composed of individuals elected by the stockholders and to whom the stockholders delegate the power to manage the corporation. (It would be impracticable for several million stockholders to directly manage IBM by committee.) It's the board of directors that makes important decisions, such as how much to pay in dividends and who shall be hired as the chief executive officer (CEO).

Net Income and Dividends

Net income (also called *net profit*) is what is left from sales after a corporation has subtracted all its costs and expenses from sales and other types of income. Dividends are declared by the board of directors and paid to the stockholders out of net income, but most corporations do not pay out all the income as dividends. They keep a healthy share of the profits in the business, for what isn't paid to the stockholders is available to spend for new equipment, advertising, and other tools for increasing net income in the next year.

More Money for the Stockholders (Capital Gains)

In addition to dividends, stockholders look for and hope for healthy increases in the market value of the stock. In the case of Soggy Boats, Incorporated (second scenario), the value of the stock increased from $10 per share to $10,000 per share in 10 years and made the owners into millionaires. During that time, the corporation paid no dividends and only minimal salaries to Alice, Bart, and Connie for their work as employees of the corporation.

It was this nonpayment of dividends and keeping all profits in the business that enabled it to buy new equipment and expand its marketing efforts. That made the stockholders far wealthier than they would have become if they had collected only dividends from a business that stayed small.

The same principle applies to publicly held corporations. It is often those that pay little or no dividends that grow most rapidly, so their stock quickly increases in value.

It is this opportunity for large gains in stock value that attracts individuals and organizations to invest in common stocks and that creates the stock market.

CAUTION

Watch Out for the IRS

There is another advantage to having your money earn money through the capital gains route: If you own for at least 18 months a stock that goes up in value, your maximum tax on the gain will be 20 percent, whereas income you receive as dividends can be taxed at rates up to 39.6 percent, depending on your total income.

Your Income from Stocks Can Be Taxed Twice

You should also be aware of the double taxation of dividends: When a corporation earns a profit, it may pay corporate tax as high as 38 percent, and it cannot deduct the dividends it pays stockholders in computing that profit. Then, when dividends are paid out of the remaining profit, the stockholder is hit with paying individual tax on the dividend, and most dividends are subject to regular income tax rates, not capital gains tax rates.

Watch the Dividend Dates

Look at what happens when the Slippery Sandpaper Corporation, or any corporation, pays a dividend:

In early June, Slippery announces that it will pay a dividend of $1 per share late in July (*payment date*) to everyone who owns its stock on July 1 (*record date*). On June 30, Arnold sells one share of stock to Betty. He thinks the stock is worth $9, but because Betty will own the stock on July 1 and receive the $1 dividend, he insists that she pay him $10. In other words, the price includes the anticipated dividend.

However, if this transaction takes place on July 2, Arnold will receive the $1 dividend, so he will sell the stock to Betty for $9. Either way, Arnold receives $10 and Betty pays $10. If the transaction takes place on July 2, she pays Arnold only $9, but she misses out on the $1 dividend. Not receiving it is, in a way, her other dollar of cost.

If Betty buys the stock for $10 on June 30, she will receive the $1 dividend in a couple of weeks, so she can think of her cost for the share as being $9. However, she views that $1 as sort of a refund of part of her purchase price which is as taxable dividend income. She is, in effect, paying tax on her own money.

The moral of this story is: Other factors being equal, buy the stock on or after the *ex-dividend* date. That's the day after the record date, so the dividend will go to the previous owner, who pays the tax, not the buyer.

EXPERT ADVICE

If the stock price is rapidly rising and you expect it will go even higher, then don't wait for the ex-dividend date. Your gain on the stock, assuming it does rise further, will offset the tax you have to pay on the dividend that is a return of your money.

These events are usually reflected in the stock price quotations. Absent other factors, the price of a stock usually drops by the amount of the dividend on the ex-dividend date.

Initial Public Offering (IPO)

Our Soggy example included an initial public offering. This term describes what Alice, Bart, and Connie did when they split the stock of Soggy and sold some of it to the public. What's so special about that? Only that sometimes the securities firm (the "underwriter") that peddles the stock to the public makes a mistake in guessing at what people will pay for the stock. If you have some investment cash available and you think the stock that is being offered to the public for the first time is going to rise quickly in market value, you would want to buy the stock when it is first issued by the corporation and the underwriter, before it has traded in the stock market. In other words, you would want to buy the stock from an initial public offering.

This tactic often works. Due to pre-offering hype and publicity, the stock does rise right after it's initially issued. Sometimes that rise is justified. (The underwriter made an error.) But it is often simply the *greater fool theory* at work. That theory goes like this: You can be fool enough to pay too much for a stock because it has had so much hype that someone else, who is a greater fool, will come along and pay an even higher price. You can sell your stock to him or her at a profit. (Avoid being the last fool in line!)

What Is and Where Is the Stock Market?

The term *stock market* describes an assortment of places and organizations, as listed later. They all operate as the basic free-enterprise icon—the auction market. If you have been to an auction house or an estate auction where you could bid on furniture, antiques, and plain old junk, you know how the stock market works. Not all stock trading is done in a physical location like an auction house (called a stock exchange by the financial community), but for this example, we'll use that scenario.

Example: Sheila owns 100 shares of Soggy Boat, Incorporated that she would like to sell if she can get at least $15 per share. Through her broker, she offers it on the stock exchange, *asking* for someone to buy it at $15. At the same time, Bill decides he would like to buy 100 shares of Soggy Boat, Incorporated, but he will not pay more than $14 a share. Through his broker, he *bids* $14 in the stock exchange. Because Sheila's *ask* price is $1 more than Bill's *bid* price, no transaction takes place yet.

In a few minutes, Carol decides she would like to buy 100 shares of Soggy and calls her broker. He checks his computer screen and tells her that the bid for Soggy is $14 and the asked is $15. Carol thinks $15 is a reasonable price, so she tells her broker to buy the 100 shares at $15. The result is that Sheila, through her broker and the exchange, sells Carol her 100 shares of stock and collects $1,500, less the broker's commission. Bill, poor guy, is left out in the cold. And he will stay out in the cold unless someone comes along who is willing to sell 100 shares of Soggy at $14 or Bill raises his bid offer to attract another seller.

It is not necessary to include a price with a buy or sell order to your broker. You can place a *market* order, which means your purchase or sale will occur immediately at the best price available on the exchange floor at that time. In the example, if Bill had placed a market order, he would have bought Sheila's stock at $15 per share.

There are several stock exchanges located in various cities. The major two are the New York Stock Exchange and the American Stock Exchange, both located in New York City. They operate in the time-honored tradition of open outcry and hand signals, and the result is as in our example.

As in this example, the buying and selling of stock is done through brokers. You cannot bid directly in an exchange unless you are a licensed stockbroker and a member of the exchange.

The market that is operated differently is the NASD (National Association of Securities Dealers), whose automated quotation service is called the Nasdaq. This market grew out of the over-the-counter system for stocks that are not listed as being eligible for trading on a stock exchange. Trading was accomplished by brokers calling each other on the telephone, but that has now been replaced by a computer system that allows every broker to know who is offering what stock at what price. The result is an auction system that operates in an auction manner, as in our example, but without the yelling and gesturing of the traditional exchanges. The NASD consists of brokers watching computer screens and making phone calls.

Stocks are usually traded in lots of 100 shares. That's because orders in multiples of 100 shares (round lots) are traded directly in the stock market, whereas lots of fewer than 100 shares have to be traded through an odd-lot broker, and that can mean higher fees and commissions.

As you are probably aware, stocks are quoted in dollars and fractions of dollars. Examples are "10⅜," which means $10.375, and 11½, which means $11.50. The reasons for this manner of quotation are couched in history, but in today's world of decimal-loving computers, it makes no sense. That is particularly so when much of the world, including our neighbor Canada, not only measures in the easy metric system but quotes stock prices in dollars and cents (a hundred cents in each dollar). There is some conjecture that the New York Stock Exchange (and, therefore, everyone else) may soon change to the dollars and cents quotation system, but old habits die slowly. In the meantime, we have to think . . . let's see, is ⅜ larger than ⅝16? . . . where's my calculator. . . ?

Any more knowledge than this about the exchanges is superfluous for most individual investors, so we'll move on.

Spread the Ownership Around (Stock Splits)

Many corporations, like Soggy Boats was before splitting up the stock, are owned by one or a few individuals. The stock is not sold to the public, and there is therefore no market for the stock. It does not matter that there are only 3,000 shares issued that are worth $10,000 each. However, when Alice, Bart, and Connie want to sell part of their stake in the company, the number of prospective stock buyers who have the cash and the inclination to purchase several shares at $10,000 is somewhat limited. As there are far more people who might be interested in shares at $10 each, the stock is split up into $10 shares.

Notice that the total value of the corporation does not change when the stock is split.

Before the stock split: 3,000 shares at $10,000 each = $30,000,000
After the stock split: 3,000,000 shares at $10 each = $30,000,000

In the real world, you are likely to find that shares of stock already publicly held and traded in the stock market will be split two for one or four for one. This is usually done to reduce the price per share so that more people can purchase the stock in 100-share lots. Such a stock split often causes the value of the new shares to be worth more than the commensurate value of the old shares. Figure 8.1 is an example of this.

The Flatten Steamroller Corporation has 1,000,000 shares of stock issued. As it is selling at a high price of $110, the management decides to split the stock in 2 (a 2-for-1 stock split).

Before the stock split:

Number of shares issued	1,000,000
Multiply by market price per share	$ 110
Market value of corporation	$110,000,000

After the 2-for-1 stock split:

Number of shares issued	2,000,000
Multiply by market price per share	$ 60
Market value of corporation	$120,000,000

Logically, you would expect that when the number of shares double the price per share would be exactly half the price of the old shares. (Half of $110, or $55 per share.) Yet, in this case, which is typical, the price of the new shares shot up to $60. The explanation is that investors and traders expect that as more people can now buy this stock in round lots, the price will be bid up in this auction market.

Figure 8.1 How Stock Splits Usually Behave

Preferred Stock

Preferred stocks are hybrids—part bond and part stock. If you own preferred stock, you will find that it acts like a bond because you usually get the same dividend checks year in and year out. That's because that's what the stock certificate says you are supposed to get, and you have to be paid that before any dividends can be paid to the type of stock (*common stock*) we have discussed up to this point. In other words, the stock is preferred as to dividends.

On the other hand, it looks like a stock because you cannot be paid any dividends until the bondholders have been paid all the interest that is due them.

There are various modifications of this basic concept of preferred stock. If you invest in any, you should carefully read the rights and obligations that go with a specific issue of preferred stock.

Convertibles

Ahhh—put the top down and the sky's the limit. So it is with convertible bonds and convertible preferred stock. A convertible security comes with the right to convert it into common stock at the option of the owner of the convertible.

Example: Fred buys a $1,000 convertible bond, paying 4 percent interest, issued by the Flatspot Tire Corporation. At Fred's option, he can turn his bond in to the corporation and receive in exchange 100 shares of common stock in Flatspot. When he buys the bond, the common stock is listed in the stock market quotations at around $6 per share.

Preferred stock can also be issued with a conversion feature, which makes the preferred stock more appealing.

A year later, Flatspot develops a process for making a tire that is guaranteed for 500,000 miles of use. The market bids the stock price up to $18 per share. Fred can now exchange his bond for 10 shares, sell them at $18 a share for $1,800, and walk away with an $800 dollar profit on his $1,000 investment. That's not a bad return in one year! Of course, if the stock doesn't rise in price, Fred still collects his interest of $40 per year. Why does Fred receive only 4 percent interest when the bond market is currently paying about 8 percent? That reduced interest is the price he paid for having the right to convert to the common stock.

Going back to the Soggy Boat, Incorporated case study (profitable scenario), Wilhemina should have insisted on a convertible feature in her bond. Then she would have shared in the good fortune of the company.

What Is the Right Price for a Stock?

This is the all-important question, but unfortunately there is no answer. There are formulas that will develop a price for a share of stock from the hard numbers on the financial reports of the corporation, but it is very seldom that the results of those formulas equal the price the stock market sets by its auction activities. These formulas go by such names as book value, return on assets, return on equity, and capitalized earnings. To describe the computation of these requires a background in financial statements and their analysis, which we don't cover here because it's a time-consuming study. (If you do want to pursue this knowledge, it's in my book, *The McGraw-Hill 36-Hour Course in Finance for Nonfinancial Managers,* published by McGraw-Hill.)

One measure of a stock's value we can describe without this background is the *price-earnings* (P-E) ratio, which is so popular a measure that it is published for each stock listed in the stock tables in the financial pages of newspapers. The example in Figure 8.2 describes how the P-E ratio is computed for two companies.

	Exploding Computer Corporation	Falling Crane Corporation
Earnings for last year	$1,000,000	$4,500,000
Divide by number of shares of		
stock outstanding	200,000	1,800,000
Earnings per share	$ 5.00	$ 2.50
Current market price per share	$110.00	$27.00
Divide by earnings per share (from above)	5.00	2.50
Price-earnings ratio	$ 22.00	$10.80

Figure 8.2 How to Compute the Price-earnings Ratio

The first requirement is to compute the earnings per share, which you do by dividing the net income for the last full year by the number of shares that have been issued that are still outstanding. (Sometimes corporations buy up their own shares and retire them, so the number issued is not necessarily the number of shares that are still outstanding.)

The second step is to divide the current market price by the earnings per share, which results in the earnings-per-share ratio.

The higher the number, the higher the market values and the higher the companies' prospects for the future. In this example, the market apparently values the computer corporation as having greater prospects for higher earnings than does the crane company.

Should You Invest in Stocks?

This is another question that is best answered with two questions:

1. Are you willing to put in the time to learn something about security analysis and how to make informed estimates of the future of various corporations?
2. Do you have enough money to invest so that you can buy stock in five to ten companies? You need to choose at least five companies, so that if one or two companies turn out to be bad choices, the other three may do well enough to keep you from going into the hole. If you buy odd lots of just a few shares of each corporation, $1,000 will get you started.

If you lack the time or the money, don't despair. You can still partake of the ownership of many dynamic businesses through mutual funds, which are covered in the next chapter.

What Are the Risks and the Non-risks? History That Is Not Taught in the Tenth Grade

If you invest in strong companies, stay invested for as long as they are financially strong, and spread your investment over several companies (*diversification*), you should expect to come out ahead of investing in bonds and other fixed investments. That doesn't mean you should sock all of your money into stocks. Part of your goal of diversified investing should be to keep a significant share of your investments in bonds and other "safe" investments. The "safe" is in quotation marks, for there is always the risk of inflation outstripping interest rates, so that your investment declines in terms of purchasing power. In fact, we have had inflation in almost every year since World War II, but we've had only three or four dips in the stock market that can be classified as serious.

"But I learned about the stock market crash of 1929 in the tenth grade. Won't that happen again?" Well, you could be hit by lightning, too, but the overwhelming odds are that you won't. In 1929 there were situations in the financial market that cannot occur again because federal law prohibits them from occurring. For instance, take the explosive situation of low margin requirements in 1929:

If you had been around in September, 1929, and decided to purchase 100 shares of Amalgamated Consolidated Corporation at $10 per share, you didn't need $1,000 to hand to the stockbroker. You needed only $100 (10 percent margin). The broker would lend you the other $900 and keep your stock in his safe as security. Obviously, if the value of your 100 shares went down to $899, the broker did not have enough security for the $900 dollars he loaned you. You could expect a phone call from him, telling you to bring in some cash to pay off part of the margin loan. (That's called a margin call.) If you and your cash failed to show up, he would sell your stock, whether or not you agreed, to protect himself.

The system worked reasonably well until a fateful day in October when stocks tumbled quickly. The brokers couldn't call customers fast enough to relay a margin call and demand cash. Customers who needed cash to meet the margin call couldn't come up with it. Normally, a customer who received a margin call would simply sell some stock on which he had a profit in order to raise cash. Now the profits in the stocks were gone. There was no source of cash.

The result of this was a spiral down. Individuals and brokers sold what little stock they had that could raise cash, but not for long. Everyone ran out of money. There were no buyers in the stock market, and stock prices almost vanished.

There were other abuses in the stock market prior to the crash. Wealthy people could manipulate the market by buying and selling large blocks of stock to make individual stock buyers think there were opportunities for profit when actually they were being fooled into investments in which they were sure to lose money.

The rules for putting together financial reports on companies were weak and almost nonexistent. Corporate controllers could put together reports that made it look as if the corporation were immensely profitable when it was really on the verge of bankruptcy. The duped public bought stock in that corporation, but the insiders knew better and sold stock when the price was bid higher. When the truth came to light, the stock price plummeted. The insiders had sold their stock, so they made handsome profits. The individuals on the outside who had bought the stock lost heavily.

Are We Protected Today from a Recurrence of 1929?

There are several laws, regulations, and rules in place that protect us from another crash like the one in 1929. Some of the reforms were instituted in the early 1930s—not long after the crash—and we are still refining the regulations and rules. Among the safeguards that now exist are these:

- You can still buy stock on margin, but you must put up at least 50 percent of the price at which you buy the stock. If the stock falls, you can expect a margin call from your broker when your margin falls to 25 percent, and some brokerage firms will make a margin call on you at a higher percentage. The 10 percent margins of the 1920s are long gone.

- The federal Securities and Exchange Commission (SEC) requires that corporate executives report all their own trades in the stock of the corporation they work for, and in some circumstances, they are prohibited from selling any such stock they own. These reports are public information, so outsiders cannot be kept in the dark.

- Corporations whose stock is publicly traded must have their financial statements audited by a certified public accountant (CPA) at least annually. Strict standards of auditing procedures developed by the American Institute of Certified Public Accountants (AICPA) must be followed by CPA firms when they audit the corporations.

- The Financial Accounting Standards Board (FASB) is a private organization that was formed to head off government regulation in the early 1970s. It promulgates rules for putting financial statements together, and all corporate financial executives must adhere to those rules if they are to pass the tests that the auditors make.

- The National Association of Securities Dealers (NASD) is another private organization that polices its own members, who are all the stockbrokers in the country. It sets standards of competency and behavior to which individual stockbrokers and brokerage firms must adhere.

In the tenth grade, they told you about the 1929 crash. They didn't tell you about today's high margin requirements, the SEC, the NASD, the FASB, and the AICPA. None of those existed, at least not with their present clout, in 1929.

Where to Go for Help in Buying Stocks

If you do have the time and a little money to invest in stocks, here are some suggestions:

- Do not start by plunging into the stock market armed only with hot tips from Uncle Harry. Blindly following advice from a stockbroker is not much better, for brokers do not have crystal balls. You need to have enough stock-picking knowledge to evaluate their suggestions yourself.
- Do educate yourself. Although many books and courses are offered, among the best and the most economical are those that come from non-profit associations.

EXPERT ADVICE

If you like group learning and a little socializing, join a local investment club. To find one, write to the National Association of Investors Corporation, P.O. Box 220, Royal Oak, MI 48068.

If you prefer to learn alone with an occasional chapter meeting, write to the American Association of Individual Investors, 625 N. Michigan Ave., Chicago, IL 60611-3110.

Both of these organizations provide excellent training materials and are not predisposed to head you toward a specific broker or investment.

Where Should You Buy Stocks?

There is a range of several kinds of places to buy stocks. Unless your television set is nonexistent, you have been barraged with advertisements of the bigger investment brokers, but you don't have to buy stocks from those people. The choices include the following.

Full-service Brokers

For the most part, these are the television advertisers, with names such as Merrill Lynch, PaineWebber, Prudential, and several others. They will offer you financial planning help, investment seminars, stock analysis reports, and many other services, which you will pay for by paying comparatively high commission rates. If you want or need such services as personal attention, some hand-holding, and advice, stop here.

Commercial Banks

Banks seem to be in the stock brokerage business these days. Bank lobbies are full of investment literature, and the larger branches have a broker installed in a private office. Actually, this operation is not performed by the bank but by a brokerage firm that is owned by the same holding company that owns the bank. The brokerage firm uses the same name as the bank with the word "Securities" appended to it.

CAUTION

You need to be aware that the funds you entrust to banks' brokerage arms do not share the insurance that covers bank accounts. Poor investments will generate a loss, which you will have to stand, just as will a poor investment in an account at an independent brokerage firm.

Again, bank brokers are a source for personal attention, hand-holding, and advice. You generally won't find a ticker tape display of up-to-the-minute stock prices. Banks tend more toward selling you package deals such as annuities and mutual funds (covered later).

Discount Brokers

There is a wide range in this category. Some discount brokers offer some discount from the commissions charged by full-service brokers and still offer some services in the form of reports on various corporations and their prospects. In short, you'll find some help but not much hand-holding.

Deep Discount Brokers

The commission structure of some of these folks (compared to that of full-service brokers) make them look as if they work for peanuts. However, their business is executing your buy and sell orders on the stock exchanges or the NASD. The assumption is that you have already done your own security analysis and know what stocks you want to buy or sell.

On-line Electronic Brokers

To use these businesses, you need a computer with a modem and, to make life easy, access to the Internet. The advantage of using these brokers is extremely low commissions. Your order is handled electronically and is almost untouched by human hands. As in dealing with deep discount brokers, you have to be your own advisor. You receive no investment advice. But if you get frustrated with computer technology and can't get your order placed, you can call for help on the computer problem or on tracking an order. The complaint you hear about these services is that, when the stock trading is heavy, you may not be able to get immediate electronic access to the firm. However, when trading is brisk, it's also hard to reach a broker in any type of firm by telephone.

Stock Trading

Our discussion of common stock investment has been slanted toward long-term investment: Pick a strong, growing company, buy its stock, and stick with that investment until conditions change, such as when the stock price goes up to an unreasonable level or the company comes upon hard times.

There is also an occupational group of *stock traders* who try to make profits by quickly buying and selling stocks as the market fluctuates, trying to hit the age-old target of "buy low, sell high." A few people are very successful at this, but most who try it fail.

EXPERT ADVICE

Should you try it? Only if you fit this picture:
- *You have thoroughly educated yourself in understanding financial statements and security analysis, just as you would for long-term investing.*
- *You have read and learned much about various strategies for short-term trading and trying to predict market trends. (No one predicts correctly all the time; you just have to do it right more than half the time.)*

EXPERT ADVICE *(CONTINUED)*

- *You understand foreign stock markets and the effect they do and do not have on the U.S. markets.*
- *You have the time to spend hours each day watching stock quotes on your computer screen. (Traders profit from swings in stock prices, and much of that fluctuation occurs during the day, not in the closing prices.)*
- *And the most important: You can afford to lose the money you use in your trading.*

CAUTION

Obviously, most people cannot meet the requirements, particularly the time requirement. If you can't meet all the listed requirements for trading, don't try it.

Derivatives

Similar to stock trading is trading in derivatives such as options, hedges, and futures. These have their place in conservative investing as protection against market fluctuations and changes in foreign currency exchange rates. Using them successfully requires in-depth education about them and the related time commitment they require. Suffice it to say that the conservative use of derivatives involves buying them in combination with the securities to which they relate. Trading in them separately without the related security and the knowledge about how to set up that relationship is pure gambling.

What's Next?

Now that we have covered what is involved in investing in individual stocks, you must be wondering how you can take advantage of opportunities in the stock market without the necessary time commitment. Actually, you may be wondering why we cover this area in a book for busy people. There are two reasons:

1. To discourage you from "taking a flyer" on Uncle Harry's hot tip.
2. To help you understand what services you are buying when management fees are deducted from your mutual fund earnings.

And those mutual funds are next.

CHAPTER

9

Mutual Funds (A Better Idea) and Other Investments

INCLUDES

- How mutual funds operate

- Where you fit into the mutual fund picture

- How you earn money from owning a piece of a mutual fund

- Why mutual funds are good for you

- A few reasons to avoid mutual funds

- How to avoid income taxes on your own money

- When the ends are closed

- Varieties and variations: real estate investment trusts, real estate mutual funds, bond funds, index mutual funds

- How to buy mutual funds

- Where to go for more help and mutual fund education

- Annuities—the improved versions may be good for you

- Gold and other precious metals—maybe a little bit of them

- Coins, collectibles, art, and similar investments (in special cases)

143

FAST FORWARD

- Mutual funds are a means for thousands of people to pool their investment funds and buy economical investment management. *(p. 146)*
- Mutual fund shares are determined by the value of the securities that the mutual fund owns, so the shares are priced at a *net asset value. (p. 148)*
- Mutual funds relieve you of having to be qualified to make investment decisions, and they provide diversification of your investments. *(p. 149)*
- Some people may not belong in mutual funds if they have sufficient resources in both money and know-how. (An individual's investing can be more flexible and specialized than that of a mutual fund.) *(p. 149)*
- Buy mutual fund shares after a distribution date so that you avoid paying tax on a distribution of your own money. *(p. 152)*
- There are special types of mutual funds for those who need special funds: real estate, bonds, index, and real estate investment trusts. *(p. 153)*
- There are plenty of sources for more in-depth help, much of it at no or minimal charge. *(p. 155)*
- Gold and other precious metals had their place during the Cold War, but the situation has changed. *(p. 160)*
- Coins, collectibles, and art are appropriate investments only if your purpose is primarily collection and investment is secondary. *(p. 160)*

Hands-on investing, whether it be in stocks of individual corporations or individual pieces of real estate, takes knowledge, experience, and much of that precious commodity, time. But time can be saved if many investors pool their investment funds and hire professional managers. In essence, that is the function that mutual funds and real estate investment trusts fulfill. As is true of any investment, investing in mutual funds requires some knowledge and time, but not what is required at the hands-on level.

This chapter covers the basics of that knowledge: the types of mutual funds, what they cost in fees, and special cases of mutual fund use, such as variable annuities.

There are buzz words in this chapter that are explained in Chapter 8. If you find unexplained terms here, please find the explanations in Chapter 8.

Mutual Funds: What They Are and How They Live

DEFINITION

The dictionary definition of mutual *is, "shared in common; joint; as, 'our mutual friend,'" and the definition of* fund *reads, "a collection of money or an appropriation to be devoted to some specific use." In the case of a mutual fund, you can think of it as the fund being the mutual friend.*

The basic concept is explained by the following example:

Example: Doris, Ernie, and Fred each has $2,000 to be invested in common stock. They could each buy two or three shares of each of five corporations, but none of the three has the knowledge required to evaluate common stocks and decide which would be the best investment. Therefore, on New Year's Day, they decide to pool their funds and hire Gretchen, who has an MBA in finance, to manage the $6,000 pool so that it generates both dividend income and capital gains. They name their pool *Swimincash.*

Gretchen opened an account for Swimincash at an investment brokerage house and selected the stocks of five companies to purchase for the pool. During the year, she spent several hours a week keeping up to date on the stocks already owned by Swimincash, as well as looking at other stocks in hopes of finding those that would generate higher income. Her efforts paid off. During the first year, Swimincash earned $800 dollars in capital gains from some profitable trades that Gretchen made, and the stocks now owned by the pool had a market value of $6,400. The pool also received $300 in dividends. The total return on the investment is displayed in Figure 9.1.

The total return on the $6,000 investment was 25 percent ($1,500 divided by $6,000). Gretchen then wrote checks to each of the three investors for $500 to distribute the $1,500 profit to them.

But now there arose a complication. Fred had come upon hard times and wanted to withdraw his investment in the pool. This was what Gretchen did: On the day she was to write a check to Fred, she added up the value of all the stocks.

Then came the problem. Gretchen had agreed to manage Swimincash for 2 percent of the fund's value. That meant she received a grand total of $150 for her work all year. That wasn't much for her year-long work, or for anybody's year of work! Gretchen wanted to resign from this management job, but she came up with a solution. She would put on her marketing hat and invite more people to put their investment funds into Swimincash—about 25,000 more. When each new member of this pool anted up $2,000, Swimincash would have over $50 million to invest, and Gretchen's 2 percent management fee would be a touch over $1 million per year. So Gretchen stayed on, hoping to attract those 25,000 investors.

Capital gain from sales of stocks	$ 800
Dividend income received	300
Total cash income	1,100
Gain in value of securities still in pool	400
Total income from investment	$1,500
Return on investment ($1,500 ÷ $6,000)	25.0%
Cash to be disbursed to investors	
Capital gain from sales of stocks	$ 800
Dividend income received	300
Total cash income	$1,100
Withdrawal from pool by Fred	
Value of stocks at end of year	$6,400
Fred's share (⅓)	2,133
Remaining for Doris and Ernie	$4,267

Gretchen had to sell stocks worth $4,267 in order to have the
cash to pay off Fred.

Figure 9.1 Swimincash, Results of First Year

Then came another problem: If, on day one of Swimincash's existence, all
25,000 investors had each put $2,000 into the Swimincash pool, it would have been
no problem to divide up the gains at the end of each year. However, some investors
had only $1,000 available, and others wanted to invest $30,000. They would all invest
at different times, and some investors would want to take their investment out of the
pool in cash. The bookkeeping would be a nightmare. Besides, offering an informal
arrangement like this to the general public would be illegal under the Investment
Company Act of 1940.

So Gretchen had Swimincash reorganized as a corporation and then jumped
through hoops, prepared mounds of paperwork, and cheered for the SEC. Then
Swimincash became a bona fide mutual fund.

A mutual fund is a corporation with the same goals, essentially, as those Doris, Ernie, and Fred had when they pooled their investment money. When you buy stock in a mutual fund, you are literally buying stock in a corporation that owns stock in many other corporations.

What Happens to the Earnings of the Mutual Fund?

Mutual funds are subject to rules unlike those that regulate most corporations that manufacture products or sell products and services. Mutual funds do not keep earnings within the corporation. They distribute the dividend and interest earnings they receive and the capital gains they generate by buying and selling stocks. Why the distribution? Mutual funds have a special dispensation from the IRS. If the fund distributes its income to the shareholders, there is no income tax levied on the corporation. (The shareholders pay their individual income tax.) That is, there is no double taxation of dividends for mutual funds, as there is for regular corporations. (Explained in Chapter 8.)

Determining the Price of Mutual Fund Shares

At the end of each day, every mutual fund adds up the market value of all the stock it owns, then divides that number by the number of shares it has outstanding. The resulting number is the net asset value. If you buy stock from the mutual fund, that figure is the price you pay. If you sell your stock back to the mutual fund, you receive the net asset value for your shares as of the night before the transaction.

Note the difference from auction markets that determine the price of shares of regular corporations. In the case of mutual funds, the auction market determines the price of the shares the fund owns, and therefore it determines the price of the fund shares, but it's done through the process described in the preceding paragraph.

Why Buy Shares of a Mutual Fund with Your Investment Money?

Judging by the popularity of mutual funds today, most investors find the following advantages to be attractive.

You Avoid Having to Make Some Decisions

You can leave the investment decisions up to professional money managers employed by the fund to make those decisions. You are probably putting in 40, 50, 60 hours a week in trying to make a living and squeeze out a little to put aside. Those working hours leave you too little time to learn and play the role of an astute investor in individual stocks, as discussed in Chapter 8.

Your Investments Will Be Spread Around

One of the keys to a successful investment program is *diversification.* If you invest all your money in one company, and a week later you hear that it is being sued for billions of dollars because its product may cause cancer, you will wish you had invested in several companies instead of just that one.

If you invest in stocks directly, there are two reasons diversification is difficult:

- If you are just starting out on an investment program, you can't do much diversifying with $1,000.
- If you do have enough bucks to diversify your investment, a single individual can keep track of but so many companies—perhaps six to 10. Mutual funds may be invested in 100 companies or more. (No, a mutual fund money manager is not superhuman, but he or she does have a staff.)

Why Many People Don't Invest in Mutual Funds

Some investors think they can do better than fund managers. (You have to educate yourself to pick a fund. Why not skip the fund and educate yourself to pick stocks?) Others prefer to avoid paying the management fees. Some want to invest in a small-niche industry with which they are familiar, and some view funds as somewhat inflexible. A couple of these reasons deserve further comment.

Fees Involved When You Invest in Mutual Funds

- Money managers, their staffs, marketing, and administrative people do not work for free. Most mutual funds charge management fees as a percentage of the funds that are managed by the fund (net assets). This can detract from the buildup of your investment.

Example: Herman studied security analysis in every minute he had available during evenings and weekends. He was certain that he could do as well picking his own stocks as could the investment guru of a mutual fund. He chose the Nevermiss Fund, one of the highest rated funds, against which to measure his own investment skills. Unfortunately, the only money Herman had to invest was his annual bonus of $1,000, but for 30 years he invested that amount at the end of every year.

The result: At the end of the 30 years, the investment return history of Herman's investment fund was identical to that of the Nevermiss Mutual Fund—14 percent. However, the fund had deducted a 1 percent management fee from its earnings every year, so it effectively earned 13 percent. The result was that Herman's investment account, which he managed himself, grew to $356,787, whereas had he invested the same $1,000 in the fund every year, he would have only $293,200—a difference of $63,587.

A 1 percent difference in management fee does make a difference.

There are also other fees that mutual funds charge:

- *Sales charges.* These are to cover the commission of the broker who sells you the shares of the fund. They're also called a *front-end loads*, which simply means that the fund loads an expense on your shoulders at the front end of your association with it. There is no need to pay a front-end load. Some funds, such as Vanguard, sell directly to the investor with little or no load, and some brokers, such as Charles Schwab Company and Fidelity Investments, also sell mutual fund shares with no load or a low load.

- *Back-end load charges.* These are charges the fund will deduct from the proceeds when you sell your shares back to the fund. If you keep the same fund shares for many years, this is not as great a concern as the front-end loads, for that charge at the end does not reduce the money you had in your fund account over the years. Also, some funds waive the back-end load charges if you stay invested with that fund for a certain number of years.

CAUTION

Be sure you check all charges a fund levies before you buy its shares. It is often the case that the no-load or low-load funds have higher management fees than do the higher-load funds. (Those fees are in the prospectus, which is a document that the fund or a broker must give you before you write a check for fund shares.)

Large Mutual Funds Are Inflexible

Big isn't necessarily better when it comes to investing in common stocks. Consider the scenario in this example:

Example: The Rubber Wrench Corporation has 1 million shares of its common stock outstanding in the hands of investors. Most of the buying and selling of these shares are in lots of a few hundred shares by individuals. The trading status at this minute looks this way:

A total of 5,000 shares are offered at $41 each.

There are bids for the purchase of 4,000 shares at $40 each.

Greg, of Greg's Mutual Fund, foresees a big market for these soft, flexible wrenches and wants to add the company to the inventory of stocks the fund owns (the fund's *portfolio*). He has decided that the time is ripe for small companies to prosper, so he wants small company stock in his fund. However, with $2 billion worth of securities in his portfolio, he is used to making *large* trades. He decides to buy 300,000 shares of Rubber Wrench at $40. His broker immediately buys the 4,000 shares that are offered and posts a bid for 296,000 shares at $40. There are no more stockholders who will sell their stock at $40, so Greg ups his bid to $41. Only 800 shares come out of the woodwork at that price. He manages to buy 1,000 more at $42, 500 at $43, and on up the price ladder. When, by his own bidding, the price is forced up to $50, he stops. He likes the stock if he can buy it at $40, but not at $50. The result is that he has been able to buy only 10,000 shares at under $50.

Obviously, if Greg is going to fill up his $2 billion portfolio with companies the size of Rubber Wrench, he is going to have to keep track of the stocks of something like 4,000 different companies.

There is no way a manager of a large mutual fund can invest much in small companies. (The jargon is *small cap stocks.*)

Buy at the Wrong Time and Pay Income Tax on Your Own Money

This is the same concept we covered in Chapter 8 under the topic of buying individual stocks after they are ex-dividend. However, you have a much bigger opportunity to run up a larger phantom tax bill with mutual funds. Here is how to do it, and more important, how to avoid it.

All year long, Greg has been buying and selling stock for his mutual fund, and most of it has generated large capital gains profits. As the year winds down in November, Greg realizes he must distribute these capital gains profits, as well as dividends the fund has received. He declares that they will be distributed on December 15 and that the distribution will be $10 per share.

On December 10, Pete receives a $1,000 holiday bonus. He immediately buys 20 shares of Greg's fund at $50 each. Then, on December 17, he receives a check from the fund for $200 (the distribution). His shares now have a net asset value of $800 ($50 per share minus the distribution of $10 per share equals the new value of $40.)

That $200 he received is taxable income to him, even though it looks as if it's just his own money being returned.

CAUTION

You can avoid making this mistake. Before you buy shares of any mutual fund late in the year, call the fund's office and find out when the distribution will be made. Buy your shares after that date.

Reinvesting that check in more fund shares does not defer the income tax on the distribution. Telling the fund to reinvest it for you so that you will never handle the money doesn't change anything. The IRS is adamant. You could have received it in cash. It is taxable income.

Closed-end Funds

So far, we have treated the subject of mutual funds as if all funds invested only in stock and as if all funds stood ready to buy their fund shares back at net asset value. As you might expect, there is an exception. It is called a *closed-end fund.* (The type of fund we have covered, in which the fund buys shares back from stockholders, is called an *open-end fund.*)

Closed-end funds are initially set up with a sale of shares to the public. When a predetermined goal is met, the fund is *closed.* No more stock is sold. Otherwise, the fund operates as does any other fund: It invests the proceeds of the sale of its shares, it collects dividends and capital gains proceeds, and distributes those to the shareholder.

Because these funds do not sell new shares to new stockholders, they do not repurchase shares from stockholders who wish to sell. Instead, the shares are traded in the stock exchanges or Nasdaq just as any stock is traded. Like other stocks, the price you pay to buy a share of a closed-end fund is set by the auction market, so it may be above or below the net asset value. That makes such funds a curiously interesting investment, but if you are new to investing in mutual funds, stick to the open-end type.

EXPERT ADVICE

Do not confuse these closed-end funds with open-end funds that have closed their doors to new stockholders. Large funds will close their sales door when they have grown so big that they have no flexibility in the marketplace.

Other Varieties of Funds

Some mutual funds specialize in holding investments other than common stocks. Except for the type of investment, they operate very much as the common stock funds do.

Real Estate Investment Trusts (REITs)

These entities operate similarly to a closed-end mutual fund and invest mainly in real estate. Like closed-end funds, they trade in the stock market. They could not be open-end because they are not liquid. They can't carry a 20-story office building onto the floor of the stock exchange and immediately sell it to raise cash for buying back a stockholder's shares. And how would you compute the net asset value? Buildings are not traded daily in an auction market.

Real Estate Mutual Funds

These funds invest in REITs, rather than directly in real estate, as well as in mortgages and operating corporations engaged in building and building supplies.

Bond Funds

Bond funds are open-end mutual funds that invest in bonds rather than in common stocks. Why not just buy the bonds directly? The bond market is composed mainly of institutions whose transactions are in the millions of dollars. An individual's order for one bond would probably be filled but at a higher cost (as a percentage of the transaction) than a large insurance company would pay. Also, nothing is 100 percent certain. A bond fund enables you to have your $1,000 diversified, for the fund owns a portfolio of bonds of many different issuers.

Some funds specialize in higher-risk bonds (often called *junk* bonds) that are issued by companies that may, but probably won't, end up in bankruptcy. Buying one high-risk bond is a foolish gamble. Buying an assortment of them moves the purchase into an investment, albeit with some risk. The likelihood that all the bonds in a high-risk fund will go belly-up is remote. If the fund loses on only a few, the higher interest rate the shareholders have shared may more than offset the few losses. If you're young and won't lose sleep over the risk, these funds can pay off in high returns. If you are fully retired, they are not the best bet for making sure your savings stay intact.

Index Mutual Funds

Index funds have grown very rapidly over the past few years. For the explanation, we have to digress into the subject of indexes. You're probably familiar with the Dow Jones Industrial Index or the Standard & Poor's 500 Index. These indexes measure the price changes in the stock of the largest U.S. corporations. Occasionally, as one company slips out of the top-of-the-heap classification and another climbs that hill, there are changes in the list of companies in the index formula but not many.

Over the years, many mutual funds have increased in value no faster than have these indexes. That raises the question: If the indexes, in which the same stocks are represented year in and year out, do as well as most mutual funds, why pay a million dollars a year or more for a mutual fund manager who regularly shifts around the fund's stock position? Why not pay an administrator a modest salary to operate a mutual fund that is composed of the same stocks that are in the index? The only security transactions would be the purchase of new stocks, in the same proportion as in the index, as new money comes into the fund from new stockholders.

This procedure has an appeal. Index funds operate with much lower fees than the usual mutual funds do, so more of your money is invested. Many people agree with that concept, for these funds are popular.

How to Buy Mutual Funds

If you have a crystal ball, buy the mutual fund shares when they are at the lowest price they will be for the next 75 years. If your crystal ball is not working properly, try what is called dollar cost averaging. For managed mutual funds, index funds, closed-end funds, individual stocks, and just about any security the price of which is established in the marketplace, dollar cost averaging works as follows.

The key is to set up a timetable for purchasing shares and to purchase the same dollar amount on the same day of every month. For instance, set up a program of investing $200 on the 20th of every month. Pay no attention to the quoted price of the stock. Figure 9.2 displays what happens. The dollar cost averaging method results in a lower cost per share than does the purchase of the same number of shares every month.

This also saves brokerage commissions.

The dollar cost averaging method does involve the purchase of fractions of shares, but almost all mutual funds can handle that. Many corporations have a provision allowing you to purchase a specific dollar amount of shares every month directly from the corporation.

Where to Go for More Help and Self-education on Mutual Funds

There seems to be more information out there than you could digest in a lifetime. However, much of it is sales promotion, so try to avoid that and seek objective help. Here are some avenues to pursue.

Same number of dollars ($200) is invested each month. The number of shares purchased each month varies with price per share.

Date	Number of Dollars Invested	Price per Share	Number of Shares Purchased
1/20/98	$ 200.00	$30.00	6.67
2/20/98	200.00	29.00	6.90
3/20/98	200.00	25.00	8.00
4/20/98	200.00	26.00	7.69
5/20/98	200.00	23.00	8.70
6/20/98	200.00	18.00	11.11
7/20/98	200.00	25.00	8.00
8/20/98	200.00	28.00	7.14
9/20/98	200.00	32.00	6.25
10/20/98	200.00	35.00	5.71
11/20/98	200.00	32.00	6.25
12/20/98	200.00	28.00	7.14
Totals	$2,400.00		89.56
Average price per share ($2,400 ÷ 89.56 shares)			$26.80

Figure 9.2 Effect of Dollar Cost Averaging

American Association of Individual Investors

625 North Michigan Avenue

Chicago, IL 60611-3110

This nonprofit organization offers many educational and information services but does not sell investments. Dues are nominal, and there is some free information at its website: www.aaii.com. (The website includes an archive of articles from the *AAII Journal* since 1991 that is available to members.)

The same number of shares is purchased every month, regardless of price per share.

Date	Number of Dollars Invested	Price per Share	Number of Shares Purchased
1/20/98	$ 210.00	$30.00	7.00
2/20/98	203.00	29.00	7.00
3/20/98	175.00	25.00	7.00
4/20/98	182.00	26.00	7.00
5/20/98	161.00	23.00	7.00
6/20/98	126.00	18.00	7.00
7/20/98	175.00	25.00	7.00
8/20/98	196.00	28.00	7.00
9/20/98	224.00	32.00	7.00
10/20/98	245.00	35.00	7.00
11/20/98	224.00	32.00	7.00
12/20/98	196.00	28.00	7.00
Totals	$2,317.00		$84.00
Average price per share ($2,317 ÷ 84.00 shares)			$27.58

Figure 9.2 *(continued)* Effect of Not Using Dollar Cost Averaging

Visit your public library and look at these services. (Call ahead to find out which branch has these services.)

Morningstar Mutual Fund Reports

Value Line Mutual Fund Survey

Standard & Poor/Lipper Mutual Fund Profiles

CDA Weisenberger

And try these websites:

The Mutual Fund Education Alliance at www.mfea.com

The Alliance for Investor Education at www.investoreducation.org

Annuities

For centuries, insurance companies have peddled a product called just plain *annuity.* An annuity works like this:

DEFINITION

Starting when you are young, you pay the insurance company a certain dollar amount every month until you are a certain age, probably 65. Then, the insurance company starts paying you back some specific amount every month for as long as you live. When you die, that ends the contract. Your heirs get nothing from a standard annuity.

There are variations on this standard annuity contract that you can buy. You pay for them by accepting less in your monthly retirement benefit. For instance, the (reduced) payments you receive in retirement can be for as long as you *or* your spouse lives. That's called a joint and survivor annuity. The annuity can also promise a specific number of payments even if you die before you collect them. That gives your heirs something if you depart this life the day after your 65th birthday.

There were two problems with this conventional annuity.

First, they came complete with the high commissions and profits that were common in insurance products until consumers became smarter.

Second, consider this scene. You were 25 years old in 1950 when $5,000 per year put you solidly in the middle class. Your friendly neighborhood insurance agent sold you an annuity that would pay you $300 a month in your "golden" years. That sounded adequate for you and your spouse when you would no longer have responsibilities for children and their education. Now you're in your 70s, happily (?) living on your Social Security and $300 per month!

Again, consumers wised up to the way insurance companies were taking expensive dollars from us and paying us back in cheap dollars. To keep this annuity business, the insurance industry developed variable annuities. Instead of basing the benefits on letting you earn only 2 or 3 percent on the money stacking up in your old-style annuity account, the variable annuity based the benefits on a common stock fund that the insurance companies maintained. That is, your benefits rose and fell with the results of the common stock fund. That was better, but it did not allow you to choose between the types of common stock investments. As befits an insurance company, they were conservative, so you were better off than in the 2 percent days but not much. And there was still a lot of commission and profit built into these annuities.

A further development has made annuities more attractive. Insurance companies are entering the mutual fund business, and even better, mutual funds are entering the insurance business. That lets you buy an annuity that, in your retirement, has the inflation protection of a common stock fund that is run by investment professionals. It also lets you choose whether you want all your annuity account to be invested in common stocks or in a balanced fund composed of common stocks and bonds. Because there are funds that concentrate in certain industries, certain countries, and other areas, you have a wide choice of what investments you want supporting your annuity benefits.

Don't malign insurance companies completely for hoarding other people's retirement money. They did one thing very well: They built a strong lobbying force that has been very effective on the U.S. Congress. Specifically, the tax law treats annuities as it does life insurance: The money you put into a stock-based annuity earns dividends and capital gains without immediate tax on those earnings. That is, all your money works for you over the years until you retire. However, the retirement benefits are taxable, and they are taxable as regular income. No annuity payout can be treated as capital gains.

The concept of never running out of money for as long as you live is appealing. If you pursue this investment route, you will find that, unless you're an actuary, it will be nearly impossible to determine how much you're paying in fees. Your best bet is to obtain several quotes on an annuity, and be sure some of the quotes come from a mutual fund.

EXPERT ADVICE

Also consider this alternative. If you are eligible to contribute to some other tax-sheltered plan, such as a 401(k), IRA, Roth IRA, Keogh, and so on, accumulate your investments there. Then, when you retire, you can use those investments to buy an immediate variable annuity. That means that you pay a lump sum for the annuity, and the payout starts the next month. The variable means that the payout depends on the performance of the mutual fund you select to be the investment inside the annuity.

Gold and Other Precious Metals

In the days of the Cold War and the possibility of a worldwide conflict between two superpowers with atomic weapons, a reserve of gold had some justification. We lived under the threat of widespread devastation and having to return to a stone-age social structure. Doughnut-shaped rocks might do as a medium of exchange, but gold would surely do better.

If you think we still live under a threat of almost complete annihilation of our society, keep some gold stockpiled. If you think the major threat has passed, gold has lost its luster. The principal problem with precious metals is that they earn no interest. Unless the price of the metal is rising at a rate faster than the interest on U.S. Treasury securities, you are losing money by holding precious metals.

Coins, Collectibles, and Art

Although you do sometimes hear stories about people enjoying phenomenal gains in the value of collectibles, art, and coins, most collectors of these items are not so fortunate. Much art that hangs on walls and many coins that lie in dusty drawers have not appreciated in value to any extent. Like gold, these investments do not earn interest. The only hope of gain is selling them at a profit.

EXPERT ADVICE

The key is that these things should not be purchased as an investment unless you also enjoy having them hanging on your wall or sitting in a display case and you enjoy the social life of meeting with other collectors. If the prospect of gain is only a secondary reason to acquire them, do they make sense?

In summary, stick with investments in stable governments and well-managed businesses, both of which provide interest and, with commensurate risk, opportunity for gains.

10

The Future— College, Retirement, and More Help

INCLUDES

- How much it will cost to educate your kids
- How to apply for financial aid
- How to put on your best "I need financial aid" face
- Types of available financial aid
- Where to find complete information on aid for which you are eligible
- Where to invest your college funds
- How the IRS helps you with college expenses (really!)
- How much you should set aside for retirement
- Where to invest retirement savings
- How to make your house into a cash-generating investment
- How to make your financial resources meet your needs after you retire
- Where to find professional help and what the initials mean

FAST FORWARD

- The cost of education is accelerating at a rate double that of the government's cost of living index. Therefore, investments for education must earn gains that are higher than that double rate. *(p. 165)*
- Start college investment when a child is very young so you can take advantage of long-term gains in the stock market. Switch to "safe" investments when the time to write checks is two or three years away. Take advantage of investments that include tax breaks, such as Series EE bonds. *(p. 165)*
- Scholarships, grants, and loans can substantially reduce the amount of money you will need for your children's college. Plan your financial affairs so that you will be eligible for that assistance. (The rules are complex and strange, and they sometimes conflict with each other.) *(p. 167)*
- While you are young, compute how much you will need in your retirement, and include a factor that recognizes the results of inflation between now and retirement. Use tax-sheltered savings plans, such as Individual Retirement Accounts and 401(k) plans. *(p. 170)*
- Take advantage of income tax credits for education: the HOPE Scholarship Credit and the Lifetime Learning Credit. *(p. 173)*
- New tax rules allow you to pull tax-free money out of your residence as you step down to a smaller house in your retirement. *(p. 175)*
- If you have already retired, change your lifestyle to conserve funds. Stay busy and prosperous—consider seasonal part-time work. *(p. 179)*

Nothing about the future is certain. In fact, the future can be scary, as witness the years we lived through the Cold War. In the field of finance, there also is nothing certain. Loan your money to the government, so it is in safe hands? What if rampaging inflation takes over, as it did in the early 1980s? Your money may be safe, but your purchasing power will have been decimated. Yet the overwhelming odds are that planning a future can bring far better financial results and happiness than not planning. We can assume that we will still live in houses and apartments, go to work most days, and receive payment for our work. Our children will need an education to survive in our technological world, and we will grow old and cease to work because of either physical infirmity or just plain burnout. The previous chapters discussed ways to keep some money for investment and the types of investments that are available. This chapter covers how much you need to carve out of your present income for the future, and some ways to reduce those needs.

Children, Smart or Not, Need Education

There used to be lots of people who were financially successful, even though they started with only a seventh-grade education, but those stories have become more rare as technology and the need for knowledge increase. Make sure your children are armed for the imminent knowledge wars.

What Is Your Child's College Material Score?

Children can be put into three categories:

- Those who are excellent students who will probably breeze through all the grades to a PhD, financed all the way by scholarships and grants. If this describes your offspring, lucky you.
- Those who are not college material. That does not imply lack of intellect or capability. Some people don't fit the college graduate mold that usually includes handling mounds of paperwork. Many who follow the education route to become skilled mechanics and artisans do far better financially than those who spend an entire career crammed into slots that do not fit them.
- Those who do fit the college mold but are average people without exceptional brainpower or quarterbacking skills. These are the offspring who will need much parental support and financial aid, as well as the willingness to provide for some of the expense through their own employment.

How Much Time Do You Have?

If Jane or John was born yesterday, probably you have 18 years in which to accumulate college money. If your son or daughter is a sophomore in high school, time is supercritical.

How Bad Is the Situation? How Much Money Will You Need?

As the years pass all too quickly, college costs rise rapidly. Rather than look at pages filled with formulas and tables, we can get a general idea by looking at four situations. But first, we need to make some assumptions about the future.

Anyone with a crystal ball or other means of knowing the future does not need this book and need not be concerned about the costs of education. The best the rest of us can do is look at the past and assume the future will be similar.

College costs have been rising approximately twice as fast as the Consumer Price Index, which reflects inflation. As inflation is currently under 3 percent, the calculations on which these examples are based assume that educational costs will increase at a rate of 6 percent (twice the inflation rate). If inflation should rise to the double-digit levels of the early 1980s, these examples would have to be recalculated.

Another assumption is the rate at which your savings will earn interest, dividends, and/or capital gains. Although the stock market in the recent past has delivered returns of 15, 20, 25, and more percent, history says this rate of return will not keep on forever. Therefore, the calculations for these examples assume a return of 10 percent on your savings. That is further refined for the tax bite by assuming a 28 percent tax bracket, and that makes the effective after-tax return to be 7.2 percent.

The costs of tuition and room and board are based on averages computed by the College Board.

The four situations are shown in Figure 10.1. For each situation, the table provides the current college cost, what the cost will be in both 15 and five years, and the monthly payment that would result in having those funds available when your child starts college—all based on the assumptions just discussed.

What Should You Do?

Those "need to save" numbers in Figure 10.1 may indicate you should live in a tent in your backyard and rent out your house. However, the zoning ordinances and your own preferences undoubtedly prohibit you from doing that. Certainly, though, you should be putting away as much as possible for your children's education, and the numbers in Figure 10.1 are goals. After all, what you set aside for this purpose is the only money over which you have control and that definitely will be available. Because how you put money aside can affect your children's eligibility for scholarships and other financial aid, we'll cover those next.

	15 Years to College	5 Years to College
Situation 1: Public, state-supported college attended by commuting from home		
Present annual cost	$ 8,100	$ 8,100
Future annual cost	19,400	10,800
Future cost for four years	77,600	43,200
Monthly saving/investment needed	187	558
Or, lump sum to invest now	18,600	26,800
Situation 2: Public, state-supported college attended as resident in college dormitory		
Present annual cost	$10,100	$10,100
Future annual cost	24,200	13,500
Future cost for four years	96,800	54,000
Monthly saving/investment needed	234	698
Or, lump sum to invest now	23,200	33,500
Situation 3: Private college, attended by commuting from home		
Present annual cost	$ 18,300	$18,300
Future annual cost	43,900	24,500
Future cost for four years	175,600	98,000
Monthly saving/investment needed	424	1,266
Or, lump sum to invest now	42,000	60,900
Situation 4: Private college, attended as resident in college dormitory		
Present annual cost	$ 21,400	$ 21,400
Future annual cost	51,300	28,600
Future cost for four years	205,200	114,400
Monthly saving/investment needed	495	1,477
Or, lump sum to invest now	49,100	71,000

Figure 10.1 Savings Needed for College

> **Assumptions:**
>
> Annual increase in college costs   6.0%
>
> Annual return on investments (after tax)   7.2%
>
> Student is resident of state in which public college located
>
> Except for monthly payment, numbers have been rounded
>   to the nearest $100.

Figure 10.1 *(concluded)*

Apply for Scholarships, Grants, and Student Loans—Lots of Them

Scholarships and other grants (money that does not need to be paid back) are not for just the superintelligent scholar and the outstanding athlete. Neither are they for students who are just under or near the poverty level. Even families with an income of $100,000 are eligible for some of this financial aid. Pursue the application process with the financial aid administrator at the college(s) of your choice.

Much of financial planning for college revolves around making your family eligible for all the help that is out there. Doing no more than filling in the financial aid forms when your student is a senior in high school will not do it. You have to "position" your finances so that you are eligible for much aid. This does not imply that you should lie on your financial aid application any more than you should lie on your income tax form. But just as you can plan your financial activities to reduce your taxes, you can plan your financial operations to increase your chances for help in the dollar department.

EXPERT ADVICE

The goal is to reduce your income and reduce your assets (things of value that you own), so that you look as poor as possible. In other words, don't grab the financial statement you gave the bank when you applied for a loan and send that off with a grant application.

Again, don't lie, but here are some ideas.

Reducing Your Income (During the College Years)

* If you are eligible for bonuses, try to have payment delayed until future years.

- Do not exercise any stock options that could result in income or an increase in assets.
- If you sell any property, such as a rental house, structure the sale as an installment sale, so that the gain from the sale is income that is spread over several years.
- If you work for your own corporation or a family corporation, have the corporation pay you a smaller salary. Make up the difference in loans from the corporation (or better, your bank) and pay them back from a higher salary after Junior or Jane graduates.

Reducing Your Assets

- Be conservative in valuing the worth of an asset, such as your business.
- If you have a significant amount of cash in the bank, use it to reduce life insurance loans or your mortgage. The reason: The cash value of life insurance and the equity in your home are not counted as assets for financial aid purposes. The best idea is to pay off the insurance loans first, because it is easy to re-borrow the money if you need it later.
- There are more ideas below, under "Where to Invest Your Savings for Education."

CAUTION

These suggestions are applicable to federal scholarship, grant, and loan programs, and to many state and private financial aid programs. However, some programs have different criteria, so be aware of that possibility.

Make Junior or Jane Independent So That Your Assets Don't Count

Just kicking Junior or Jane out of the house will no longer make him or her independent in the eyes of the grant and scholarship committees unless he or she is over 24, is a veteran, is married, has a dependent, or is enrolling in graduate school. If one of these exceptions applies, and your student does not have much in the way of income or assets, this is a good maneuver to obtain more financial aid.

What Is Available in the Form of Grants and Scholarships?

A list of just the names of available scholarships would take up many pages and not be of much use, but there are sources of current information.

College Financial Aid Directors

These are the professionals who work in this field. Give them the opportunity to help line up financial aid by contacting them early. Make college selections early in the junior year of high school so that you can apply for scholarships before any deadlines.

Financial Planners

Be sure any financial planner you engage has a thorough knowledge of this field. It's almost as complex as the income tax law, and, like the tax rules, there are contradictions. (Example: Assets in a child's name can save you some income tax when the child is young but will reduce your financial aid profile when he or she starts college.)

CAUTION

Not all personal financial planners are well informed in this area. Use a fee-only planner. Some "college-aid" planners use the service as a front to sell insurance and annuities (which aren't counted as assets) for a commission.

To evaluate your planner and control the money you're paying him or her, do a little self-education first. Suggestions for that follow.

The Internet

Several Internet sites offer information. Some of them cost money and some of them are free. Try these sites:

- www.fastweb.com
  This free site will ask for much information about your student, your family, occupation, associations, and other facts. Then it will match your profile to its database of scholarships and provide a list of those for which your student may be eligible.

- www.finaid.org
  This free site is sponsored by the National Association of Student Financial Aid Administrators (NASFAA) and contains about 75 subheadings covering the financial aid field.

- www.yahoo.com
  In this search engine, go to "Education" on the menu, then click on "College Entrance." From the resulting menu, click on "Financial Aid" for more sites you can visit. The list includes more interactive sites such as Fastweb, and many of the sites are by reputable organizations, such as the College Board.

If you don't have Internet access, you may be able to access it at your public library or through a friend's computer. Or do this: Help your student to buy one while in high school by borrowing the money from the bank and working part-time to pay it off. You will have to co-sign, but it will start your student toward obtaining credit and will be one less purchase to make when college starts. Don't just loan your money to Junior or Jane. A missed payment to Mom or Dad is just (ho-hum) a missed payment. A late payment to the bank puts the student into a sweat, just like any adult with the temporary "shorts."

Books

Scores of books cover this subject in much more detail than would fit in this one. Visit your library or bookstore, or visit an on-line bookstore. For example, visit "www.amazon.com" and find the search window. Enter the words "financ aid college" for a comprehensive list of books. (Use the partial word "financ" so you will retrieve both "finances" and "financial.")

Where to Invest Your Savings for Education

Do not put your savings for education into simple investments such as a bank's certificates of deposit. There are investments that, in effect, make the IRS pay part of your education expense through some tax breaks.

Individual Retirement Accounts Can Be Used for Education

If you can have *all* your dollars, instead of just your after-tax dollars, earning income, you won't need to save as much out of your current income. If you are eligible to invest in an IRA, it is a means of keeping all your money working and earning income until you need it for college bills.

Series EE Bonds

United States government Series EE bonds accumulate (accrue) the interest each year you hold them, but there is no income tax to pay until they mature or you cash them in. However, if you use the proceeds for education, you never pay income tax on the interest earned over the years you hold the bonds. In other words, if you use them for education, these EE bonds become similar to tax-exempt municipal bonds. At 6 percent interest, they are equivalent to 8.3 percent if you are in the 28 percent tax bracket and 8.7 percent if you are in the 31 percent tax bracket.

CAUTION

Avoid this trap: When you cash in these bonds, the income is tax-free, but it is still income for the purposes of financial aid. The solution: Do not cash your EE bonds until after you have submitted the financial aid form for your student's senior year.

Pay Down Your Mortgage

One of the best ways to save for college is to apply your college savings money to paying off your home mortgage, which will mean you can borrow more on a home equity line of credit. Why? The federal student loan and grant programs do not consider the equity in your home as an asset, so on the financial aid application you look poorer than you are. When you need cash for college, borrow it against the line of credit.

EXPERT ADVICE

A line of credit is preferable to a second mortgage that would dump a lump sum in your pocket. If you put that lump sum in a bank account, it would be an asset, which makes you richer and less likely to receive financial aid.

Stocks, Bonds, and Mutual Funds

Properly chosen, these are good investments for college funds. Except for U.S. Treasury Series EE savings bonds, they offer no special features or tax advantages as educational savings. However, if financial aid application time is imminent and you have any unsecured consumer debts, such as credit card balances and signature loans, do this: Use your securities as collateral for a new loan from a bank or from your securities broker, and use the proceeds to pay off the unsecured debt. The reason for this action is that most financial aid formulas do not allow a reduction of your worth for unsecured debt, but they do add the stocks, bonds, and mutual funds to your worth. However, if stocks, bonds, and mutual funds are collateral for the debt, only their net value is included in your worth. In other words, you will look poorer if you follow this procedure.

Example: Loretta has $500,000 invested in mutual funds. She also has credit card debt and unsecured signature loans that total $250,000. The financial aid formula will ignore the debt and consider her as an individual with a net worth of $500,000, which may make her ineligible for aid for her son's education.

Wanda has the same financial picture, but she borrows $250,000 secured by her mutual funds, from her broker and pays off the credit cards and signature loans. The financial aid formula will now list her mutual funds as having a net value of only $250,000, so her chances of financial aid are now much better than are Loretta's.

Employers' Retirement Plans, Annuities, and Life Insurance

These investments are designed primarily for your retirement, not for college funding. However, they do have an impact on college funding, because financial aid formulas usually do not count the value of these plans in determining your total assets. They can also be a source of college funds when everything else runs out, providing you can borrow from these plans.

Some Help from the IRS (Really!)

There are some tax breaks for students and their parents, as follows.

Income Tax Credits

The Taxpayer Relief Act of 1997 provides for two credits for educational expenses. Credits subtracted from the tax (not your income) are equivalent to receiving a check from Uncle Sam.

The HOPE Scholarship Credit

To be eligible for HOPE credit, the student must be enrolled at a post-secondary institution on at least a half-time basis. The credit can be claimed for only the first two years of education, and the maximum is $1,500. (100 percent of the first $1,000 and 50 percent of the next $1,000). You can claim this credit for each student if you have more than one in the first two years of post-secondary education. ("Post-secondary" is the buzz word, and it includes trade schools if the school meets certain requirements.)

The Lifetime Learning Credit

This tax credit is 20 percent of up to $5,000 of expenses for post-secondary education, for expenses paid after June 30, 1998. In 2003, this limit rises to 20 percent of up to $10,000 of expenses. You can claim this credit only once each year, no matter how many offspring you have in post-secondary education.

Both of these credits are phased out as your income rises over $40,000 on a single return or over $80,000 on a joint return. You can claim only one of these credits for each student each year. And there's another kicker: The expenses used to compute these credits must be reduced by the amount of any scholarship that is not taxable income, as well as by the amount of most government educational assistance to members of the armed forces and veterans.

Interest on Higher Education Loans Is Deductible

As is your mortgage interest, this interest is deductible from income in computing adjusted gross income. You can deduct this interest and still claim a standard deduction in lieu of itemizing deductions. (Applicable if you are renting your home or your home is paid for.) The deduction is limited to $1,000 in 1998, but it rises to $2,500 over the four years to 2001, and it is phased out for incomes over $40,000 ($60,000 for joint returns).

The law also prohibits double-dipping. If you use a home equity loan to finance education and you deduct the interest as home equity interest, you cannot also deduct the same interest as education loan interest.

No Penalty for an Early Withdrawal from an IRA for Education

Normally, if you withdraw funds from your IRA before age 59½ you have to pay a 10 percent penalty. However, if you use the funds for higher education, there is no penalty. (You still pay income tax on the proceeds unless the funds are in a *Roth IRA* or an *education IRA.*)

What Your Offspring Can Contribute

Summertime employment and perhaps some part-time work during school can help, but don't wait for the college years to look for your child's contribution. Junior's or Jane's income may reduce the available financial aid by almost as much as the student earns during the college years. If the financial aid is in the form of loans, the student's working may be a good idea, for it will cut down the post-college debt. If the aid is in the form of scholarships or grants, that work may result in almost no gain to the family.

However, savings from your student's employment during the high school years can help. During the ninth grade, make it clear that the college status symbols and luxuries come out of your scholar's pocket, not yours. Even though it will probably be a requirement, list the laptop computer along with the stereo as a luxury. If an automobile is required for commuting to class, put that burden on your student also.

EXPERT ADVICE

Use your student's cash for these so it won't show up as an asset on the financial aid application.

Will You Ever Retire? How Will You Live? How Long Will You Live?

What will your retirement be like? The conventional picture today is that of working 40 to 60 hours per week until, one fine day, you stop. You go home. You have no more boss (spouse excepted), no more schedules, no more meetings, and no more stress.

But: There may be no more money! That may mean you work until later in life, or you work at a less demanding job, or at a seasonal job.

What Will Be the Source of Your Income?

Your retirement income will, you should hope, come from more than one source.

Social Security: Retirement for (Almost) Everyone

Yes, there are cries that Social Security is going broke, and that is true. Undoubtedly, though, Congress will somehow rescue it. It may include a "needs test," which means that only those who qualify as relatively poor will receive Social Security. Or it may be that the age at which you are eligible to receive Social Security is pushed even further than the current threshold of 67 (for those born after 1959). So Social Security may provide you with some income, and it may not.

EXPERT ADVICE

In the meantime, make sure your earnings record in the giant Social Security system computer is accurate. At least every three years obtain a copy of your record by calling Social Security at 1-800-772-1213.

Pensions

Pension plans that often guaranteed you a specific number of dollars each month in which you were retired are disappearing. It may be just as well. If you were to retire today, a pension of $40,000 per year could allow you to live comfortably. However, 20 years from now, after the effects of inflation, that income could be near the poverty level.

Earnings on Investments

If you have been wise in your pre-retirement years, you have accumulated some investments in mutual funds or variable annuities. If after retirement you continue to keep a balanced investment portfolio, you should be able to keep up with inflation, as you could not with the conventional fixed pension.

Cash from Your Home

As you made mortgage payments for many years, you built up your equity, or investment, in your home. There are ways to pull cash out of that equity.

Reverse Mortgages

When you enter into one of these arrangements, the scenario goes like this: When you retire, you will have paid off your mortgage and any home equity loans you may have had. Now, you again mortgage your house, and in return you receive money. You can take the money as a line of credit, giving you some flexibility. You can take it as a fixed amount of money every month for a specific number of months. When you reach that number, the payments stop, and you then may have cash flow problems. Or you can arrange for a specific lower amount to be paid to you until you die, as long as you live in the house. There are some disadvantages to obtaining cash this way:

- There are significant fees involved in the reverse mortgage, that eat into the cash you squeeze out of your house.

- If you decide to move after a few years, the mortgage company gets paid back all the money it advanced you, plus interest. There may be little left for you.

- The payments you receive are for a specific amount. As prices creep up with inflation, you will become unhappy with the diminishing buying power of the monthly checks.

Sale of Your House

There is a better alternative: Sell your house and buy (or rent) a smaller one. After paying for the smaller house, put the cash left from the sale into an investment such as a balanced mutual fund. If you prefer guaranteed payments until you die, purchase a variable annuity that starts monthly payments right away (immediate annuity). There used to be a tax disadvantage to this if you made a habit of selling your house and buying a less expensive one, but that went away with the Taxpayer Relief Act of 1997. Now you pay no tax on capital gains on the sale of the residence if the gain is under $500,000 (on a joint return), and you can take advantage of that rule every two years. That lets you and your spouse sell your large family house in Boston, retire to a smaller house in New Hampshire, and when you become too old to enjoy the snow, sell it and buy a tiny house in Florida—all without sharing a penny of the sales proceeds with the IRS (up to $500,000 on each house). That cash is yours to invest.

Why would you bother with being tied into a reverse mortgage, complete with heavy fees?

How Much Do You Need to Put Away for Your Retirement?

Figure 10.2 is a computation of retirement needs for Joe, who is 20 years away from retirement. The income part is covered in the previous section. Most of the expenses are self-explanatory, but a few deserve some explanation.

- The *travel expense* is not a monthly expense. It is more likely to be an infrequent expense of a much larger figure. The $500 a month in this computation makes sure that the $6,000 per year is available whenever it is needed.

- The *asset replacement* item is similar. You may think that your automobile will last until you are 95, when the Department of Motor Vehicles says "walk" and snatches your license away. Don't believe yourself. The car will wear out and you will get new-car fever in retirement just as you did when you were working. Putting this item in the computation makes sure you will have the necessary cash when that time comes.

- The *net investment return rate* is a little more complex. In this case, Joe expects that he will earn 10 percent on his investments during his retirement. Out of that the IRS will take its cut, so we estimated that 20 percent of the 10 percent return (which equals 2 percent of the total investments) would go to income taxes. Inflation is a similar tax. If inflation is 3 percent per year, you have to reinvest at least 3 percent of your total investments to keep them growing as fast as inflation. In other words, Joe cannot take that 3 percent out and spend it. He has to reinvest it. So the 2 percent for taxes and the 3 percent for inflation are deducted from the 10 percent return, leaving a net return (which can be taken out in cash) of 5 percent.

- The *investment that will yield annual shortfall* is the amount of money that Joe will have to have invested at 5 percent to generate $14,400 per year. You can compute this by dividing the annual cash needed by the rate of return ($14,400 ÷ 5% = $288,000).

- The *monthly investment to accumulate $288,000 in 20 years* is computed by a complex formula. Rather than do that, ask your friendly broker or banker to compute it for you on a financial calculator.

Monthly income:		
Social Security	$1,200	
Pensions	1,500	
Annuity payouts	100	
Reverse mortgage	0	
Total monthly income		$ 2,800
Monthly expenses:		
Income tax	100	
Rent or house payment	700	
Maintenance	100	
Utilties	150	
Property taxes	55	
Telephone	50	
Cable/satellite	45	
Medicare supplemental insurance	200	
Long-term care insurance	500	
Casualty insurance	200	
Groceries	300	
Eating out	200	
Automobile expenses	200	
Entertainment	200	
Travel	500	
Asset replacement	500	
Total monthly expenses		4,000
Short fall (income minus expenses)		(1,200)
Annual shortfall		($ 14,400)
Net investment return rate		5%
Investment that will yield annual shortfall (Shortfall ÷ net return rate)		$288,000
Monthly investment to accumulate $288,000 in 20 years		$ 553

Figure 10.2 Computation of Retirement Needs

The Future Is Here

What if you are already retired, your picture is like Joe's, and you don't have the $288,000? Don't despair, but think about these solutions.

Squeeze Money Out of Your House

If you have money tied up in a big house and the family has all left the nest, take money out of it, as already discussed, and invest it.

Fill in Your Free Time with Temporary or Part-time Work

At this writing, labor is in short supply. Some software companies are training retirees to fill computer-related jobs, including systems analysis and programming.

Mail résumés, make phone calls, and answer ads. Don't put your age in your résumé, but don't hide it either. For the six-figure pressure-cooker job, age discrimination still exists, although it is well hidden, but who wants one of those jobs anyway? Employers hire retirees for mid- and low-level jobs because they want employees who are flexible as to work schedules and seasons (for example, tax return preparation). Retirees want flexible work that allows downtime for travel and other pursuits. There are matches for those needs. You just have to find them.

Don't overlook the possibility of a minibusiness—something you can do in the spare bedroom or the garage. Preferably, it should be one you can put on hold for weeks on end when it's travel time. It can consist of consulting, writing, woodworking, or whatever fits your nature.

Change Your Lifestyle

When you sell your house, don't automatically expect that you must invest at least $100,000 of the proceeds in another one. There are retirement communities with lower-priced condos.

Consider ridding yourself of all the expenses of a house by purchasing a livable RV. That lets you move around and stay in the "great weather" belt year round. (Rent an RV and try it out before you make that move.)

And Later On . . .

Eventually, it may be necessary for you to move to a long-term care facility. That may take whatever money you have left, but Medicaid will, we hope, catch you and all of us. That subject was covered at the end of Chapter 4.

Where to Go from Here? Do You Need Professional Help?

After you have digested what's in this book and looked at a few other sources of information that were recommended, you may still need the help of a professional financial planner. The person you should choose for that job depends on your needs. When you talk to a financial planner about using his or her services, cover at least these points:

- What your needs are, such as investments, tax planning, financial aid for college, estate planning, and so on.
- Ask about the planner's experience with the areas of your need.
- How is the planner compensated? Is it by the fee you pay or the commissions on investment products he or she recommends. (Find a planner who is compensated only by the fee you pay. It will be cheaper for you than paying high commissions on financial products the planner sells you.)
- How are fees charged? By the hour or by the task?
- Will the planner provide only the information you want or insist on a full-blown analysis of your situation? Those full-blown analyses can run on for many pages and cost thousands of dollars. They are appropriate for a wealthy person but not for someone who just wants help in starting an investment program with $100 a month.

Most financial planners have some initials after their names. Here's a rundown of the most common and what they mean.

- Certified Financial Planner (CFP). This designation indicates that the individual has a bachelor's degree or more than five years of financial planning experience plus a specific course of study in financial planning at a university. In addition, the CFP must have passed a 10-hour examination, have work experience in financial planning, and adhere to a specified course of ethics.
- Certified Public Accountant (CPA). This designation is earned by individuals who have a college degree with a concentration in accounting and tax courses, who have passed a rigorous 2½-day exam, and who have

experience in the accounting field. They must adhere to a prescribed code of ethics. If you are self-employed or an owner of some part of a small corporation, you should involve a CPA in your planning. Note, though, that not all CPAs are knowledgeable in investments and insurance. However, if they also have a designation as a Personal Finance Specialist (PFS), which is awarded by the American Institute of Certified Accountants, they can advise you on the full range of financial planning.

- Chartered Financial Consultant (ChFC). People with this designation have completed 10 courses in financial planning, meet specific experience requirements, and maintain ethical standards. You are most likely to find this designation appended to the name of an insurance agent.

- Chartered Life Underwriter (CLU). These people have completed courses and exams in the life insurance area. They may or may not be knowledgeable about investments and taxes. As indicated by the name of the designation, most holders of this designation are insurance agents.

- Registered Financial Planner (RFP). The holders of this designation must have completed a course in financial planning and have some experience in financial planning.

- Lawyers. Most lawyers have a four-year college degree plus a degree from a law school and have passed a rigorous examination for admittance to the bar (to practice law). The lawyer whom you might engage for financial planning will also have an advanced degree in taxation and may well be a CPA. If your wealth exceeds $625,000, this is the individual who can help you avoid the onerous federal estate tax. (You may still need someone else for advice as to specific investments.) Obviously, someone with these credentials will be expensive, but if your heirs could be hit with estate tax, it could be money well spent.

In Conclusion

Have your financial goals in mind. Do your homework by reading the basics of the planning areas you need to pursue. Then buy the advice to make sure your plan is achievable.

See you on Easy Street.

Appendix

Tax Rate Table
(For Determining Tax Bracket)

Step 1: Find your 1997 federal income tax return and look at the figure for taxable income on page 2. That determines your tax bracket as follows:

	Your tax bracket percentage is:
If you are single and your taxable income is:	
Not over $24,650	15%
Over $24,650 but not over $59,750	28%
Over $59,750 but not over 124,350	31%
Over $124,650 but not over $271,050	36%
Over $271,050	39.6%
If you are a married couple, filing a joint return, and your income is:	
Not over $41,200	15%
Over $41,200 but not over $99,600	28%
Over $99,600 but not over $151,750	31%
Over $151,750 but not over $271,050	36%
Over $271,050	39.6%
If you are married and filing a separate return, and your income is:	
Not over $20,600	15%
Over $20,600 but not over $49,800	28%
Over $49,800 but not over $75,875	31%
Over $75,875 but not over $135,525	36%
Over $135,525	39.6%
If you qualify for head-of-household rates and your income is:	
Not over $33,050	15%
Over $33,050 but not over $85,350	28%
Over $85,350 but not over $138,200	31%
Over $138,200 but not over $271,050	36%
Over $271,050	39.6%

If your income falls near the taxable income that divides one tax rate from another, you may have to calculate some of your tax savings or cost at one rate and some at another rate.

Figure A.1 Determination of Your Tax Bracket Percentage for Calculating Federal Income Tax Effects

Computation of Interest Rate in Equipment Lease Contract

Instructions for Using Table in Figure A.2 for Estimating Interest Rates

Take the monthly rental you are quoted and divide it by the cost of the appliance or other equipment. Then multiply that result by 100. Look for the resulting payment in the body of this table. Find the nearest payment number and look to the first column on the left to find the approximate interest rate you are being charged.

Example:

You can rent a refrigerator with a cash price of $700 for $30 per month. At the end of 30 months, the rental company will transfer title of the refrigerator to you. What is the interest rate you are paying?

$30 ÷ $700 =		0.0429
Multiply by 100		$4.29

Look under the 30-month column, find the closest payment, which is $4.31. The left column shows that the interest rate is approximately 21 percent.

If you make a down payment or security deposit, deduct that from the cost of the appliance before making the foregoing calculation. (You do not pay interest on your own money.)

For automobile leases, the computation is more complex. You can view the lease as two loans. One is an installment loan for the depreciation of the value of the automobile over the term of the lease. The other is an interest-only loan for the residual value. You can use trial and error to find an interest rate that fits the payments for the installment part and the interest for the residual part. A better idea is to find a friend who has a loan amortization program on a computer or a financial calculator (if you don't have one yourself). Use the amortization program for a loan with a balloon payment. The residual is the balloon. Also, if you're a user of a power spreadsheet, you can use the formula for internal rate of return to compute the interest involved.

Payments for number of months on $100 loan							
Interest Rate	**12 Months**	**18 Months**	**24 Months**	**30 Months**	**36 Months**	**48 Months**	**60 Months**
6%	8.61	5.82	4.43	3.60	3.04	2.35	1.93
7%	8.65	5.87	4.48	3.64	3.09	2.39	1.98
8%	8.70	5.91	4.52	3.69	3.13	2.44	2.03
9%	8.75	5.96	4.57	3.73	3.18	2.49	2.08
10%	8.79	6.01	4.61	3.78	3.23	2.54	2.12
11%	8.84	6.05	4.66	3.83	3.27	2.58	2.17
12%	8.88	6.10	4.71	3.87	3.32	2.63	2.22
13%	8.93	6.14	4.75	3.92	3.37	2.68	2.28
14%	8.98	6.19	4.80	3.97	3.42	2.73	2.33
15%	9.03	6.24	4.85	4.02	3.47	2.78	2.38
16%	9.07	6.29	4.90	4.07	3.52	2.83	2.43
17%	9.12	6.33	4.94	4.11	3.57	2.89	2.49
18%	9.17	6.38	4.99	4.16	3.62	2.94	2.54
19%	9.22	6.43	5.04	4.21	3.67	2.99	2.59
20%	9.26	6.48	5.09	4.26	3.72	3.04	2.65
21%	9.31	6.52	5.14	4.31	3.77	3.10	2.71
22%	9.36	6.57	5.19	4.36	3.82	3.15	2.76
23%	9.41	6.62	5.24	4.41	3.87	3.21	2.82
24%	9.46	6.67	5.29	4.46	3.92	3.26	2.88
25%	9.50	6.72	5.34	4.52	3.98	3.32	2.94

Figure A.2 Table for Estimating Interest Charged in Lease/Purchase Agreement

Sources of More Information

Katt, Peter C. *The Life Insurance Fiasco, How to Avoid It.* Dolphin Publishing, 1992

Baldwin, Ben G. *The Complete Book of Insurance.* Irwin Professional Publishing, 1996.

Scott, David L. *Wall Street Words.* Houghton Mifflin, 1988 (This is a very useful 395-page glossary of all financial terms. It's not limited to the stock market.)

Index

A

A. M. Best Company, 60
Accident-related disabilities, 44, 47
Accident-related insurance, 44, 47, 64
Accountants, 137, 180
After-tax interest rates, 29–30
Alliance for Investor Education, 157
Alternatives, less expensive, 2, 7–8
American Association of Individual Investors, 138, 156
American Institute of Certified Public Accountants, 137, 180
American Stock Exchange, 130
Annual fees, credit cards, 12, 14
Annuities, 158–159, 172, 175
Anticipated needs, 11
Appliances
    lease/rental of, 37–38, 184–185
    maintenance of, 19–23
    purchase of, 9
Art, 144, 160
Ask price, 129
At-risk rules, 31
ATM charges, 81–82
Attorneys, 181
Auctions, stock, 122, 129, 133, 148
Automobiles
    expenses, 5–8, 35–37

Automobiles—*Cont.*
    insurance for, 22, 78
    lease of, 26, 32–37, 184
    loans for, 35–36
    purchase of, 26, 32, 34–37

B

Back-end load charges, 150
Balloon mortgages, 98–99
Bank fees, 76, 81–83
Bank money market accounts, 83–84, 88
Banks
    emergency funds in, 76, 80–83
    loans from, 26, 29, 78–79
    as stockbrokers, 139
Bathrooms, 4
Beneficiaries, 51
Bid price, 129
Blue Cross, 67
Boards of directors, corporate, 126
Bond funds, 144, 154
Bondholders, 119, 125
Bonds, 171–172
    convertible, 119, 133
    corporate, 5, 7, 106, 118–119, 125
    municipal, 97, 106, 116–118
    savings, 106, 108–112, 118, 162, 170–171

Bonds—*Cont.*
    state, 97, 106, 116–118
    Treasury, 106, 113–114, 118
Borrowing, 26–41, 76, 78–79
Briefcases, 14–15
Bureau of Public Debt, 116
Buying, versus leasing, 26, 32–38
Buying Treasury Securities, 116

C

Capital gains, 127
Capital gains taxes, 127
Cash flow, 100–101, 103
Cash value, 55–57
Cash-value life insurance, 54–57
CDA Weisenberger, 157
CDs (certificates of deposit), 83, 88
Cellular telephones, 4, 14–15
Certificates of deposit (CDs), 83, 88
Certified financial planners (CFPs), 180
Certified public accountants (CPAs), 137, 180
CFCs (chartered financial consultants), 180–181
CFPs (certified financial planners), 180
Charge accounts, revolving, 26, 28–29
Charles Schwab Company, 150
Chartered financial consultants (CFCs), 180–181
Chartered life underwriters (CLUs), 181
Checking accounts, 81–82
Closed-end funds, 153
Closed-end leases, 34
CLUs (chartered life underwriters), 181
COBRA benefits, 64, 71

Coins, 144, 160
Coinsurance, 66–68, 72, 78
Collateral, 26, 29, 96
Collectibles, 144, 160
College education, 162, 164–174
Commissions
    insurance agents, 44, 57, 60
    real estate agents, 95–96
    salespersons, 33
    stockbrokers, 122, 138–139, 150
Common stocks, 121–141
Consumer loans, 26, 29–30
Consumer Reports, 72
Continuation-of-benefit rules, 64, 71
Controls on money, 26, 38–41
Conveniences, 4–6
Convertible bonds, 119, 133
Convertible stocks, 119, 133
Convertible term life insurance, 53
Corporate bonds, 5, 7, 106, 118–119, 125
Cost-of-living adjustments, 47
CPAs (certified public accountants), 137, 180
Credit cards, 2–3, 12–14, 26–27, 29, 76, 78–79, 85–86
Credit lines, 26, 31–32, 76, 78–79, 171
Credit unions, emergency funds from, 76, 82
Creditors, 125

D

Damaged merchandise, 16
Dealers, maintenance contracts from, 21
Death benefits, 54–57

Decreasing term life insurance, 54

Deductibles

    maintenance contracts, 22–23

    medical insurance, 66–68, 72, 78

Deductions

    401(k) plans, 40–41

    interest on student loans, 173

    itemization of, 29–31

Deep discount brokers, 139

Deferred needs, 10–11

Depreciation, 99–101

Derivatives, 122, 141

Disability insurance, 44–51, 61

Disaster insurance, 76–79

Discount brokers, 139

Discounting, 115

Discretionary expenses, 39–40

Disease-related disabilities, 44, 47

Disease-related insurance, 44, 47, 64

Distributions, 144, 148

Diversification, 135, 144, 149

Dividends, 122–128, 132

Dollar cost averaging method, 155–157

Dow Jones Industrial Index, 154

Duff & Phelps, 60

E

Earnings, protection of, 43–61

Easy-payment plans, 28

Economic activity, 10

Education, 32, 162, 164–174

Education IRAs, 170, 173

Education loans, 32, 162, 167–168, 173

Elimination period, 47

Emergencies, 75–88

Emergency funds, 76–88

Employer-provided disability insurance, 49

Employer-provided medical insurance, 64–66, 68–71

Employer-provided retirement plans, 172, 175

Employment

    retiree, 178–179

    student, 172–174

Equipment (*see* Appliances)

Equity loans, 26, 29–32, 78–79, 171

Essentials, 2, 4–6, 10–12, 32, 38–39

Estate taxes, 58–59

Estimated taxes, 17–19

Ex-dividend dates, 128

Excess charges, medical expenses, 66–68

Expenses

    appliances, 9

    automobiles, 5–8, 35–37

    briefcases, 14–15

    buying/selling home, 95–96

    cellular telephones, 14–15

    on credit cards, 13

    discretionary, 39–40

    education, 32, 165–167

    equity financing, 30–31

    essential, 39–40

    fixed, 39–40

    furniture, 28

    medical, 32, 66–68, 72–73

    public transportation, 7–8

    retirement, 176–178

F

Family doctors, 69
Federal Deposit Insurance Corporation, 80, 107
Federal Reserve banks, 110, 115
Fee for Service, 59
Fee-only advisors, 44, 57, 60
Fidelity Investments, 150
Finance charges, credit cards, 12–13
Finance companies, loans from, 26, 29
Financial Accounting Standards Board, 137
Financial aid directors, 169
Financial planners, 169, 179–181
Financial planning, 3
Financing, 26–41
Fixed expenses, 39–40
Fixed rate mortgages, 97–98
Food costs, 10
401(k) plans, 40–41, 58–59, 159, 162
Front-end load charges, 150
Full-service brokers, 138
Furniture, 28

G

Gatekeepers, at HMOs, 69
Gold, 144, 160
Government bonds, 106–118
Government programs, inadequacy of, 44–46, 64, 72–73, 91, 174
Grace periods, credit cards, 12–13
Grants, 162, 167–170
Greater fool theory, 129

Group disability insurance, 49
Group health insurance, 70–71
Group life insurance, 60

H

Health care, 63–74
Health insurance, 32, 58, 63–74, 78
Health maintenance organizations (HMOs), 64, 68–70, 72–73
HMOs (health maintenance organizations), 64, 68–70, 72–73
Home, purchase/sale of, 95–96, 176
Home equity financing, 26, 29–32, 78–79, 171
Homeowner insurance, 78, 94
HOPE Scholarship Credit, 162, 172–173

I

Illness-related disabilities, 44, 47
Illness-related insurance, 44, 47, 64
Impulse purchases, 2, 10–14
Income
   net, 126
   present, getting more out of, 1–23
Income tax credit, 162, 172
Income taxes, 39, 50, 59, 117, 127, 148, 152
Index mutual funds, 144, 154–155
Individual retirement accounts (IRAs), 56, 59, 159, 162, 170, 173
Inflation, 93–94, 102, 106–108, 113, 135, 165, 175

Inflation-indexed bonds, 106, 113–114

Initial public offerings (IPOs), 128–129

Insurance

automobile, 22, 78

disability, 44–51, 61

disaster, 76–79

health, 32, 58, 63–74, 78

homeowner, 78, 94

life, 31, 44, 51–61, 172

long-term care, 64, 73–74

maintenance contracts, 19–23

medical, 32, 58, 63–74, 78

mortgage, 54

supplemental medical, 64, 72–73

tenant, 78, 94

Insurance companies

annuities from, 158–159

disability insurance from, 46–51

disaster insurance from, 78

health insurance from, 66–68, 70–71

life insurance from, 52–57, 59–60

Interest earned

bonds, 5, 7, 106–117, 119

CDs, 83

money market accounts, 83

money market funds, 84–85

savings accounts, 82

and taxes due, 16–19

Interest paid

consumer loans, 26, 29

credit cards, 13–14

education loans, 173

home equity loans, 26, 29–32

Interest paid—*Cont.*

leases/rentals, 38, 184–185

mortgages, 31, 96–99

retail stores, 26, 28–29

Internal Revenue Service, 2, 16–19, 31, 94, 100, 127, 148, 152, 172, 176

Investment, defined, 87

Investment clubs, 122, 138

Investor associations, 122, 138, 156

IPOs (initial public offerings), 128–129

IRAs (individual retirement accounts), 56, 59, 159, 162, 170, 173

J

Junk bonds, 119, 154

K

Keogh plans, 59, 159

L

Late charges, credit cards, 13

Laundry costs, 9

Lawyers, 181

Leasing, 26, 32–38, 184–185

Level-premium term life insurance, 53

Life insurance, 31, 44, 51–61, 172

Life Insurance Advisers Association, 59

Life insurance agents, 59–60

Lifetime Learning Credit, 162, 172–173

Lipper Mutual Fund Profiles, 157

Loans, 26–41

    automobile, 35–36

    consumer, 26, 29–30

    education, 32, 162, 167–168, 173

    emergency, 76, 78–79

    home equity, 26, 29–32, 78–79, 171

    mortgages, 27, 31, 94, 96–99, 171, 175

    restructuring of, 26, 29

Long-term care insurance, 64, 73–74

Long-term investments, 90–103

Luxuries, 2, 4, 11–12, 38–40

M

Maintenance contracts, 19–23

Major expenditures, justification of, 2, 9

Major medical policies, 64, 68

Manufacturers, maintenance contracts from, 21

Margin calls, 136–137

Market orders, 130

Means tests, 74

Medicaid, 74

Medical care, 63–74, 78

Medical expenses, 32, 66–68, 72–73

Medical insurance, 32, 58, 63–74, 78

Medicare, 64, 72–74

Medicare HMOs, 64, 73

"Medigap" insurance, 64, 73

Merrill Lynch, 138

Mileage, 33, 35

Money market accounts, 83–84, 88

Money market funds, 84–85

Moody's Investor Services, 60, 118

Morningstar Mutual Fund Reports, 157

Mortgage insurance, 54

Mortgages, 27, 31, 94, 96–99, 171, 175

Municipal bonds, 97, 106, 116–118

Mutual Fund Education Alliance, 157

Mutual fund fees, 150–151

Mutual funds, 36, 83–85, 135, 143–157, 171–172, 175

N

Nasdaq, 130

National Association of Investors Corporation, 138

National Association of Securities Dealers, 130, 137, 139, 153

National Association of Student Financial Aid Administrators, 169

Necessities, 4–6, 10–12, 38–39

Need-to-have items, 2, 4, 10–12

Negotiation, in shopping, 2, 16

Net asset value, 144, 148, 153

Net income, 126

Net pay, 39

Net profits, 126

New York City bonds, 118

New York Stock Exchange, 130–131

Nice-to-have items, 2, 4, 11–12

Nonessentials, 2, 4–6, 11–12, 38–41

Nursing homes, 64, 73–74

O

On-line brokers, 139–140
Open credit lines, 76, 79
Open-end funds, 145–153
Open-end leases, 34
Opportunity costs, 5
Orange County, California, bonds, 118
Over-the-counter trading, 130

P

Pagers, 4
PaineWebber, 138
Partial disability, 48
Passbook savings accounts, 82
Payment dates, 128
Pension benefits, 45, 47
Pensions, 175
Personal finance specialists (PFSs), 180
PFSs (personal finance specialists), 180
Planning, financial, 3
Plumbing, 4
Portfolios, 151–152
Pre-existing medical conditions, 64, 70–71
Preferred stocks, 132–133
Premiums
    credit cards, 14
    disability insurance, 47–50
    health insurance, 64, 66, 71
    life insurance, 52–56
    maintenance contracts, 22–23
Present income, getting more out of, 1–23

Price-earnings ratio, 134
Prices, stock, 129–134
Primary care physicians, 69
Prime share accounts, 82
Priorities, need to set, 2, 4–9
Profits, net, 126
Prudential, 138
Public transportation, 7–8

Q

Quotations, stock, 130–131

R

Real estate, 89–103
Real estate agents/brokers, 90, 95–96, 103
Real estate investment trusts (REITs), 103, 144,
    153–154
Real estate mutual funds, 144, 154
Record dates, 128
Refinancing of mortgages, 98–99, 171
Refunds, tax, 16–17
Registered financial planners (RFPs), 181
REITs (real estate investment trusts), 103, 144,
    153–154
Related-party transactions, 31
Renewable term life insurance, 53
Rental management companies, 102
Rentals
    appliances, 37–38, 184–185
    real estate, 90, 94–95, 99–103

Repairs, 19–23, 34, 36

Restructuring of loans, 26, 29

Retailers

    maintenance contracts from, 21

    revolving charge accounts with, 26, 28–29

Retiree employment, 178–179

Retirement, 162, 174–179

Retirement plans, 172, 175

Reverse mortgages, 175

Revolving charge accounts, 26, 28–29

Rewards, need for, 38–40

RFPs (registered financial planners), 181

Risk, from bonds/stocks, 106, 108, 119, 122, 135–137, 140–141, 154

Risk tolerance, 92–93

Roth IRAs, 56, 59, 159, 173

S

Safe investments, 105–119, 135

Sale items, 10–11

Savings accounts, 82

Savings bonds, 106, 108–112, 118, 162, 170–171

Savings plans

    appliance maintenance, 19–20

    college education, 165–167

    emergencies, 79–80

    and life insurance, 55–56

    nonessentials, 11–12, 39–41

Scholarships, 162, 167–170

Secondary securities market, 114–115

Securities brokers, 114, 117–118

Securities and Exchange Commission, 137

Self-employed individuals, 59, 65

Self-motivation, 38–41

SEP plans, 59

Series EE bonds, 106, 109–112, 118, 162, 170–171

Series HH bonds, 106, 110–112, 118

Services, reductions in, 2, 14

Share draft accounts, 82

Shares, 123–125, 144, 149, 153

Shopping, improvements to, 2, 16

Short-term investments, 87–88

Short-term stock trading, 122, 140

Small cap stocks, 152

Social Security, 44–47, 58, 74, 91, 174

Social Security Administration, 46

Social Security taxes, 39, 50, 58, 72

Speculative ventures, 108

Splits, stock, 131–132

Standard & Poor's, 60, 118, 157

Standard & Poor's 500 Index, 154

State bonds, 97, 106, 116–118

Statement savings accounts, 82

Stock exchanges, 129

Stock market crashes, 122, 136–137

Stock markets, 122, 127, 129–131, 135–137

Stock prices, 129–134

Stock quotations, 130–131

Stock splits, 131–132

Stock trading, 122, 140

Stockbrokers, 122, 130, 137–140

Stockholders, 122, 125–127

Stocks, 171–172

    common, 121–141

Stocks—*Cont.*
    convertible, 119, 133
    preferred, 132–133
Straddle interests, 31
Student employment, 173–174
Student loans, 32, 162, 167–168, 173
Supplemental medical insurance, 64, 72–73
Supplemental Security Income, 93

T

Tax breaks, for education, 162, 172–173
Tax credits, 162, 172
Tax percentage rates, 30
Tax rate table, 183
Tax refunds, 16–17
Tax-deferred savings plans, 40
Tax-exempt bonds, 97, 116–118
Tax-exempt income, 31, 117
Taxes
    and bonds, 106, 110–114, 116–117
    capital gains, 127
    and disability insurance, 48–50
    estate, 58–59
    estimated, 17–19
    income, 39, 50, 59, 117, 127, 148, 152
    and interest paid, 26
    itemization of deductions, 29–31
    and life insurance, 56, 58–59
    and money market funds, 85
    and mutual funds, 144, 148, 152
    and net pay, 39

Taxes—*Cont.*
    overpayment of, 2, 16–19
    and real estate, 90, 94, 96–97, 99–103
    Social Security, 39, 50, 58, 72
    and stocks, 122, 127–128
    withheld, 17–19, 39
Taxpayer Relief Act (1997), 172, 176
Telephones, 4
Tenant insurance, 78, 94
Term life insurance, 51–56
Time, value of, 2, 7–8, 14–15
Travel, credit cards for, 12, 27
Treasury, U. S., 114–116
Treasury bills, 88, 106, 113, 115
Treasury bonds, 106, 113–114, 118
Treasury inflation-indexed bonds, 106, 113–114, 118
Treasury notes, 106, 113, 118
Treasury securities, 109, 111, 113–116, 160

U

Universal life insurance, 56–57
USAA, 60

V

Value Line Mutual Fund Survey, 157
Variable life insurance, 56
Variable rate mortgages, 97–98
Veritas, 60
Video telephones, 4

W

Wall Street Journal, 114
Warranties, 19, 21, 34
Weiss, 60
Whole life insurance, 56

Withheld taxes, 17–19, 39
Worker compensation, 46

Y

Yield, 114–117, 119

About the Author

Robert Cooke is a Certified Public Accountant with extensive experience in the areas of tax, personal finance, and business planning. He has explained the basics of these areas in many seminars presented across the country as well as in columns for national publications. He has also written several books on finance and taxes, including *The McGraw-Hill 36-Hour Course in Finance for Nonfinancial Managers*.